Business Decisions

*...the impact of corporate mergers and
global capitalism on our lives*

About the author

Larry J. Eriksson is a consultant and writer residing in Madison, Wisconsin. He has previously served as an engineer, manager, corporate officer, and corporate director at several major corporations as well as a number of smaller companies. Dr. Eriksson received his B.S.E.E. from Northwestern University, his M.S.E.E. from the University of Minnesota, and his Ph.D. from the University of Wisconsin-Madison. The author of many papers on technology and management with numerous U.S. and foreign patents, he is a Fellow of the Society of Automotive Engineers and the Acoustical Society of America. In addition to his professional activities, he enjoys reading, biking, golfing, swimming, practicing his violin, and playing with his grandchildren.

About the publisher

QUARTER SECTION PRESS publishes nonfiction, fiction, and poetry with a special emphasis on themes related to building a more sustainable, just, and humane world. Its name recalls the 160 acres or quarter section that comprised the typical small, family farm in the years following the Homestead Act of 1862.

Business Decisions

*...the impact of corporate mergers and
global capitalism on our lives*

Larry J. Eriksson

QUARTER SECTION PRESS
a unit of Eriksson Research, LLC
Madison, Wisconsin, U.S.A.

Disclaimer
The statements in this book are
the personal opinions of the author based on his experiences
as a corporate engineer, manager, officer, and director.

Author's Note
This book includes material from the author's unpublished memoir,
*Managing to Live...the impact of corporate mergers
on people, businesses, and communities.*

First edition

10 9 8 7 6 5 4 3 2 1

Printed on acid free paper.
The text is set in 11-point Times New Roman font.

ISBN 0-9721875-0-2

Library of Congress Control Number: 2002092680

QUARTER SECTION PRESS
a unit of Eriksson Research, LLC

6105 Fairfax Lane
Madison, WI 53718-8262 U.S.A.

608.222.2689
erikssonresearch@execpc.com
www.execpc.com/~erikres www.madisonconsultants.com

❧ *Contents* ❧

vi

Figure Captions

To my grandchildren
and their generation

Note to the reader

The text often makes reference to an article, report, or book. The section entitled *Chapter Notes and References* at the end of the text contains a listing under the appropriate page number of these references with their authors. The *Bibliography* contains the complete citation.

◈ *Acknowledgments* ◈

Writing any book is a major undertaking. I completed this book on a snowy evening almost exactly four years after I left the corporate world. The process of writing sharpened my views of corporate mergers and global capitalism. It also helped me to work through my personal feelings as I entered a new stage in my life. I owe a particular debt to my family. My children and grandchildren continue to inspire, amaze, and support me. They have all contributed to this book in many ways both small and large.

This book evolved from my experiences in the corporate world as well as a wide variety of books and articles listed in the bibliography. Numerous discussions with friends and relatives were also very helpful. Special thanks are due to Bonnie Block, John Peck, and John Rowe for reading the manuscript and providing many stimulating comments and questions. In particular, the detailed editorial review of the final manuscript by my son, Mark Eriksson, generated many thoughtful comments that have improved the clarity and precision of the writing.

Most importantly, the completion of this book is due in no small part to the continual encouragement and support of my wife, Karen Eriksson. In addition to her love and understanding, she has made invaluable contributions to the form and content. She has critically read numerous drafts, suggested many improvements, and served as a sounding board for many ideas.

June, 2002

Larry J. Eriksson
Madison, Wisconsin

✂ *Preface* ✂

The small church would not have looked out-of-place in a New England village. Red brick with white trim, it was on the outskirts of Stoughton, a Wisconsin community well-known for its Norwegian heritage. A short distance up the road from the church was the headquarters of Nelson Industries, a manufacturing company that had called Stoughton its home for nearly sixty years. The surrounding fields had been farmland until the recent growth of Nelson and the Stoughton community had replaced cornfields with office buildings and houses.

Inside the church, a scattering of Nelson shareholders sat quietly in the church pews listening to the terse proceedings. The only topic on the agenda was to vote on the sale of the company. It was January 8, 1998 -- the last day of Nelson's existence as an independent company.

* * *

Despite their claims to improving productivity and efficiency, corporate mergers and global capitalism are creating significant personal and societal costs throughout our country and the world. Economic consolidations are turning many communities and even entire countries into virtual colonies of absentee corporate owners. Wisconsin provides a good example of a once powerful economic region that, due to corporate mergers, is increasingly dependent on decisions made in distant board rooms to determine its economic future. Consequently, employees and local communities are struggling to deal with a radically changed economic landscape.

For nearly 25 years, I served as the Vice-President of Research at Nelson Industries, Inc., a medium sized manufacturing business based in Stoughton, Wisconsin, about ten miles southeast of Madison. During that period, Nelson produced acoustical noise control and filtration products at a network of manufacturing plants located in small towns throughout Wisconsin as well as in Canada, Mexico, and Europe. In my position as Vice-President of Research, I also cofounded and served as an officer and director of Digisonix, an intrapreneurial startup owned by Nelson in the emerging field of electronic sound cancellation.

I was an integral part of the corporate world for most of my professional life and the recipient of the various benefits that it has to offer. I saw its strengths and weaknesses. Over the years, I experienced changes and problems as a normal part of the life of any organization. I recognized that hard decisions are sometimes necessary in operating any business. However, the new and supercharged version of global capitalism that has emerged over the past several decades has created a corporate climate that is fundamentally different from the business world that I knew as a young engineer. The dominance of this new business perspective has profoundly affected all aspects of our lives. My recent experiences have compelled me to write this book to critique these changes and the effects of the numerous corporate mergers that have occurred.

In January of 1998, the Cummins Engine Company, a major supplier of diesel engines and related equipment headquartered in Columbus, Indiana, purchased Nelson Industries including its subsidiary, Digisonix. Nelson and Digisonix became part of the Filtration business unit of Cummins that also included

Fleetguard, a leading manufacturer of filtration products for engines. I became the Chief Technical Officer of the Fleetguard/Nelson unit with continuing responsibilities for Nelson Corporate Research activities in Stoughton as well as new responsibilities for Fleetguard engineering activities in Cookeville, Tennessee and several other locations.

Over the years, Cummins has received recognition at the national level in a number of business rankings. Some years ago, Levering and Moskowitz listed Cummins in their book, *The 100 Best Companies to Work for in America*. More recently, *Business Ethics* magazine included it in the top ten companies on their list of the 100 best corporate citizens. However, despite these accolades, I found that the world of the large corporation and the changes that came with my new position were inconsistent with my personal goals and desires. I resigned and created a new lifestyle that better met my personal needs.

Other employees also had a difficult time adjusting to the impact of the merger on their lives. In addition to my concerns for these employees, I thought about the impact that various corporate mergers and deregulated global capitalism were having on our local communities as well as our greater society. As a parent and grandparent, I worried about the implications for my children and grandchildren.

How will the loss of corporate headquarters and declining employment opportunities in our local communities affect their lives? What will be the effects of ongoing job changes, business reorganizations, and cost reduction programs on their careers? How will they respond to growing economic uncertainty in their lives? How will they and their families cope with the ever increasing demands of tighter deadlines, e-mail overload, round the clock meetings, and ever more burdensome travel?

On a larger scale, how will the continuing loss of economic diversity and small businesses affect our local communities? What will be the long term effects of corporate mergers on our country? Where is our seemingly unbounded enthusiasm for the business paradigm and market system taking us? Why do we allow economic considerations to dominate virtually all of our decisions? What will be the consequences of growing disparities in economic power and wealth? What do our answers to these questions say about our fundamental values and priorities?

This book considers these questions and many others that our aggressive form of global capitalism raises for all of us. It tries to help those directly affected by mergers, whether through loss of employment or changing working conditions, to better understand the underlying causes of corporate actions and see new ways of viewing their experiences. It also provides new perspectives on how we can better manage our companies and make more informed decisions. In particular, it presents younger workers, who have only known a world dominated by mergers and aggressive global capitalism, with a view of business and management that is rapidly becoming a fading memory. Finally, the book suggests alternatives to enable society to address the problems that corporate mergers and aggressive capitalism present for our local communities and the global economy.

As a professional and manager in the corporate world for over 30 years, I have gained considerable experience with many different forms of organizations including small businesses, global corporations, high tech startups, and nonprofit organizations. Although large corporations and organizations are essential to meeting some of the critical needs of our society, I believe that we have neglected the special strengths and contributions of small businesses. We have become overly enamored with large enterprises and growth.

My views on small businesses grow out of my years at Nelson and Digisonix as well as my experiences in forming two small businesses, one before and one after my work at Nelson. I also grew up in a family in which self-employment and small businesses were a way of life. My father was self-employed throughout most of his working life during which he organized and operated three tool and die shops. Members of my extended family have formed more than a dozen small businesses including machine shops, manufacturing businesses, a northern Wisconsin resort, a real estate business, a log home company, a Web-based sales business, an auto restoration business, a consulting business, and a drive-in restaurant.

Small businesses are the foundation of our economy and offer a variety of advantages for our communities. Corporate mergers and consolidations have ended or threatened the future of many of these small businesses. My personal experiences will guide an exploration of small business culture and a comparison with the culture of the large corporation. The unique management style and culture found in many small businesses suggest new approaches for the effective management of companies of all sizes.

Today, many people are writing about the impact of economic changes on our society. They sometimes suggest that these changes and the resulting problems are the inevitable consequence of the development of new technology. Although technological change is a powerful force, we have been living with the industrial revolution for two hundred years and the development of specific new technologies for much longer.

Instead of looking at technology as the source of our problems, this book views our economy in the context of the various decisions and choices that we make -- and are often made for us by others. It challenges our excessive confidence in the market system to guide our society. It emphasizes the need for individual initiative as well as collective action to respond to our problems. It presents specific proposals on how we can build a society that is more humane and inclusive -- a society in which the focus is on people rather than numbers.

The title of the book, *Business Decisions,* stems form the tendency of current managers to justify corporate actions as simply "business decisions." Unfortunately, as we will see, these decisions often result from quantitative financial analyses that are incomplete and take a short term perspective. We need to take a more expansive view of our business decisions as well as those decisions that we make in our personal lives.

Those outside of the corporate world may find the analysis of global capitalism in this book too kind. Those within the corporate world may find some proposals too extreme. Nonetheless, many people in both groups are beginning to recognize the need for change, the need to reform the ways we conduct our businesses and run our lives. We need to find a middle ground where we can recognize both the real contributions and the significant problems of large scale capitalism and the current global economy.

CHAPTER 1

Mergers in Wisconsin

It was Thursday, December 4, 1997. Tension and anticipation filled the air as 300 Nelson employees filled the large meeting room. The subsequent announcement of the company's proposed sale stunned most of the employees and managers. After so many years of rumors, it was hard for many to believe what they were hearing or to understand what it would mean. As they slowly returned to their offices, they found it difficult to return to their usual work. Although things still looked the same, they knew that their world in Stoughton, Wisconsin, a small community just thirty minutes southeast of Madison, would never be the same.

* * *

The Story of a Small Business

• The early years

During the 1930s, Dr. C. F. Burgess was a noted electrical and chemical engineering professor at the University of Wisconsin. In addition to his university research, Dr. Burgess had great interest in commercializing his research activities. As a result, he formed the Burgess Laboratories. This was long before the era of research parks and high tech spin-offs from modern research universities. Today, numerous Midwestern companies trace their origin to early work at his laboratories.

One of the areas Burgess investigated was the use of unusual materials such as the fibers from cattail plants for acoustical purposes. Blankets made from these fibers, rolled into tubes, and inserted into metal cans formed a sort of primitive acoustical silencer. These and other experiments in acoustics and silencers led to the creation of a small muffler business at Burgess Laboratories.

In 1939, Charles "Pete" E. Nelson, Edwin "Ed" E. Bryant and Oscar "Ockie" F. Gusloff bought this embryonic muffler business from Burgess and moved it to an automotive garage in Stoughton, Wisconsin. The Nelson Muffler Corporation began its business as a manufacturer of acoustical products, including exhaust mufflers for trucks, tractors, and motorcycles. Many heavy duty and off-road vehicles at this time had little, if any, muffling of the engine exhaust noise and so there were many opportunities in this area. Nelson developed a reputation as being able to supply custom designed quality mufflers in relatively low volumes at competitive prices.

Nelson was a small company that both encouraged and required individual initiative. No large staff groups existed either to provide support or to create bureaucratic hurdles. Employees had to take personal responsibility for a project. The management was usually decisive and encouraged good ideas. The resulting environment was attractive to action oriented individuals -- especially those who were familiar with the constraints of larger organizations.

As part of a relatively small company, employees worked on a wide range of activities including product sales, manufacturing, and engineering. Nelson also encouraged employee involvement in outside professional activities. Over the years, Nelson employees participated as leaders in a wide variety of technical societies and trade associations.

The atmosphere was friendly and informal. The company held coffee breaks in the hallway and everyone participated from the president to the newest employee. Meetings often included eating together or at least sharing a cup of coffee and perhaps a donut. Business lunches at local restaurants, overlooking nearby Lake Kegonsa, would lead to informal meetings with other groups from Nelson.

On New Year's Eve, the employees would celebrate together after work in the basement lunchroom of the Stoughton office building. In the summer, there were picnics at local parks. Each fall brought traditional Norwegian lutefisk dinners at a local Lutheran church. The annual shareholder meeting including a buffet lunch, and various holiday parties contributed to a friendly, cooperative atmosphere.

Despite the collective hard work and commitment to improving and growing the company, most employees were always able to find time for themselves, their families, and their communities. There were occasional breakfast meetings, more often luncheon meetings, and sometimes evening dinner meetings with the board of directors or visiting customers. It wasn't unusual for managers to spend a few hours catching up on some reading or other work a few evenings each week or over the weekend. However, most employees rarely missed dinner with their families and had time to attend events with their children as well as serve in their churches and local communities. They enjoyed their jobs, led a balanced life, and, in most years, the company continued to grow and prosper.

In 1972, following the untimely loss of its two senior managers, Nelson was at a critical point in its history. New noise control regulations were creating demands and opportunities for the company to expand its capabilities. Foreshadowing the future, the company chose to go outside the firm to hire several new senior executives who initiated a number of new programs and activities. I joined Nelson in 1973 as Director of Research to establish a new Nelson Corporate Research Department. A few years later, the Nelson board elected me Vice-President of Research.

As part of this process of renewal, the Nelson Muffler Corporation changed its corporate name in January of 1974 to Nelson Industries, Inc. This name provided an umbrella for Nelson's non-muffler businesses that were becoming increasingly important, including industrial silencers supplied by the Universal Silencer division, filtration products supplied by the Nelson Filter division, and later, computer services supplied by its subsidiary, Professional Data Processing (PDP).

The company was entering an exciting era. It had a new name, new management, and many new opportunities. The corporate management and board were progressive and open to new ideas. They encouraged employees to develop innovative technology, products, manufacturing, and marketing programs.

In 1979, Nelson celebrated its 40th anniversary. As part of the celebration, teams of supervisors presented every employee in virtually all of its locations, essentially on the same day, with a satchel of 40 dollar coins. These coins were no longer real silver as they had been 15 years earlier at the company's 25th anniversary, but with about 1000 employees, the number of coins was tremendous and the total weight almost overwhelming. In fact, it was no small task to even obtain so many dollar coins from the banks. The personal impact was great, the symbolism powerful, and the linkage to the past inescapable. It was another good example of the type of team building that is possible in a smaller company.

• Recession and innovation

In the early 1980s, the steady success of the company suffered a temporary reversal. A severe recession began for Nelson, as well as much of the so-called rust belt, creating new challenges for the company. In 1983, the company lost money. The appraised value of the company's stock fell sharply. Throughout this difficult time, the company remained focused on retention of its work force and maintenance of programs critical for the future. Despite shared belt-tightening and increased budget controls, Nelson continued to pursue new technology and products. Today, many firms look to these expenses as the first to be reduced. Nelson shareholders took a long term view of their investment in the company and supported efforts to prepare for the future.

During this difficult period, there were no widespread layoffs or salary reductions. The company wanted to take advantage of future opportunities by retaining its labor force. Justifying this confidence, sales did rebound sharply in 1984, and the company entered a long period of sustained growth, as did much of the economy.

Occasionally, the management team traveled as a group to visit other Nelson facilities. One of these trips to Europe included a visit to a muffler plant constructed as part of a license agreement that Nelson had with a large Austrian manufacturing company. This plant was near the head of a valley high in the mountains that had a history of heavy manufacturing that went back to the beginnings of the iron age. Unfortunately, over the years, the local industry had diminished, and the area's residents now had rather limited employment opportunities.

One of the local managers vividly described their plight as the bus wound its way through the mountains in the growing dusk of a late afternoon. He began a long and emotional soliloquy on the plight of these workers and the importance of this muffler plant to their lives and those of their children. The Nelson managers could readily identify with his thoughts and concerns.

At the time, Nelson's relatively small plants were in small communities scattered throughout western and northern Wisconsin and northern Ontario where good manufacturing jobs were hard to find. Larger firms would usually not locate small plants in so many dispersed locations, yet it made good business sense. Nelson enjoyed the benefits of readily available, skilled employees. The small, rural communities benefited from well paying manufacturing jobs.

In the early 1980s, Nelson Industries combined its Nelson Muffler division and Nelson Filter division into a single Nelson Division ostensibly to create a stronger company. Many years later, employees heard similar arguments when the shareholders approved the sale of the company. It is a common assumption whenever organizations merge.

However, mergers may not only multiply the combined strengths of both organizations, but also their combined weaknesses. It is usually easy to determine the potential benefits that might accrue through the combination of two businesses. It is more difficult to identify the sometimes subtle disadvantages that also result from the combination. For example, the filter division was one of three relatively independent business units that had comprised Nelson Industries. The company now had one less division and fewer separate departments. While this may have reduced costs to a certain extent, it also reduced the product focus inherent in more specialized business units, and it reduced opportunities to develop new managers.

Despite the consolidation of the muffler and filter divisions, it was more common at Nelson to follow a pattern of business formation and separation. Many years earlier, Burgess Laboratories was a spin-off from university research. Nelson, in turn, was a spin-off from Burgess. Over the years, a number of other businesses could similarly trace their roots back to Nelson or Burgess. The result was a modest web of companies connected through history and products. Continuing this trend, work soon began that would lead to the formation of one of the most widely known businesses created by Nelson.

At this time, personal computers were bringing some of the power of mainframe computers within reach of the average consumer. For businesses, personal computers offered a number of opportunities to improve traditional business practices and products through the use of tools such as spreadsheets, computer-aided drafting, and data acquisition systems. However, powerful microprocessors soon led to a new technology that had the potential of changing the very nature of the mufflers and silencers that Nelson produced. This technology was the electronic cancellation of sound, also known as active sound control. It became clear to a number of Nelson managers and directors that this technology presented both a potential threat and opportunity for the company.

In 1982, in order to study this emerging field and with the encouragement and support of Nelson, I returned to school to complete my Ph.D. at the University of Wisconsin-Madison. It was a good example of how the flexibility of a small company enabled a senior manager to pursue a personal goal that also met the immediate as well as the long term needs of the company. During the next several years, working with my advisor and other graduate students and Nelson employees, we developed important innovations in active sound control technology. These new developments soon formed the basis for several new product lines and business opportunities for Nelson.

In 1987, Nelson formed a new business unit, Digisonix, to commercialize the new technology and products. Due to demands for additional space to house its growing staff and product development activities, it soon moved into a former tractor dealership just a short walk from the Nelson Technical Center in Stoughton. Although this building was quite old and barely adequate in many ways, the location was a great advantage due to the intense interactions at this time between the Digisonix staff and research engineers at the Nelson Technical Center. Physical proximity is a great way to bridge organizational boundaries that isolate groups from each other. Its importance became even more evident many years later after Nelson became part of a much larger organization.

Nelson gradually received recognition as a world leader in the emerging field of active sound and vibration control. Nelson researchers published numerous technical articles and papers, and general interest articles mentioning this work began appearing in such respected publications as *The New York Times, Time,* and *Science.* Major development activities began with a number of companies, including the Ford Motor Company, which led to the opening of a new joint development center in Madison, and the Lord Corporation. In late 1992, reacting to its technical and commercial successes in active sound control, Nelson management decided to make Digisonix a wholly owned subsidiary with headquarters in a new facility in Middleton. Digisonix entered a period of rapid expansion of both its staff and facilities.

➤ Support of small businesses

Digisonix would never have existed without the commitment of Nelson's management to the exploration of new technologies and the development new products. This commitment led to a broad range of support for active sound control research and Digisonix that included:

- early management support and initial funding;
- use of existing facilities and equipment;
- expansion of staff as required;
- investment in new facilities and equipment;
- technical, manufacturing, and administrative support;
- relationships with outside suppliers;
- introductions to existing customers;
- continued encouragement from senior management; and
- ongoing funding for the development of the business.

A small, entrepreneurial company, managed for long term success and without the pressures felt by many publicly traded corporations to produce short term financial results, can accomplish great things. Most Nelson shareholders had substantial familiarity with the company and took a long term perspective. The management could pursue programs that took years rather than focusing on the next quarter's results.

➢ Benefits from small businesses

As a result of this support, a small number of Nelson employees were able to create technologies and products that led to new business opportunities in active sound and vibration control as well as other areas. Some of the specific benefits of this technology and Digisonix for Nelson included:

- a portfolio of new technologies and patents;
- new opportunities in the company's core businesses;
- new product lines for sound and vibration control;
- access to new customers, markets, skills, and facilities;
- additional technical depth to support other activities;
- an incubator for managerial and technical talent;
- experience with new management practices;
- an increased emphasis on technology and innovation;
- development of a more competitive spirit;
- incentives to create new passive silencing products;
- additional revenue from development contracts;
- increased expectations for success; and
- an enhanced image as forward looking and progressive.

The story of Nelson and Digisonix demonstrates the way in which a smaller corporation or business can create economic diversity within its organization through the formation of small units. As we will see, the contributions of Digisonix and other smaller units within Nelson parallel the way in which smaller businesses benefit our overall economy and society.

• The end of an era

Nelson celebrated its 50th anniversary in 1989 as a prosperous, successful company. Reflecting the growing size of the company, this anniversary did not include any silver dollars. However, as part of the celebration, the company published a corporate history that included a review of the company's progress in technology. Unlike the current tendency of many corporate managers to discount the past as irrelevant, Nelson's history continued to be a source of pride for many of its employees and managers.

By the 1990s, Nelson's traditional business was accelerating, the stock market was beginning its long boom, and Nelson continued to produce excellent financial results. This made the company attractive to potential purchasers as interest in mergers was growing throughout world. Prospective purchasers approached Nelson to discuss the possible purchase of the company, but there was no immediate financial pressure to sell the company.

However, there were a number of non-financial issues facing the company. A number of board members and senior managers were approaching retirement age. In addition, as a privately traded corporation with a relatively small number of shareholders, the liquidity of the company's stock as well as its long term capital needs were topics of continuing discussion. Furthermore, many mergers were occurring throughout the automotive parts industry. Among the reasons driving these mergers were the movement of large companies towards fewer suppliers, a concern over being too small to compete, and a fear of being left behind.

All of these factors led to continual speculation as to whether another company would purchase Nelson. Many employees discounted these rumors as idle speculation and did not expect to learn of a sale in the foreseeable future. In fact, Nelson often reiterated that although the company was gathering information related to the continuing wave of mergers that were occurring, it preferred to remain private and independent.

Nonetheless, in the first week of December in 1997, Nelson announced that it had received a cash offer to purchase the company. On the following Saturday, Nelson Industries held its annual meeting at the new Monona Terrace convention center overlooking Lake Monona in downtown Madison. The highly regarded architect, Frank Lloyd Wright, created the unique design that was the inspiration for this building, and it would have ordinarily dominated discussions. However, that would not be the case at this meeting. Nelson's existence as an independent company was soon to end.

Following the initial formalities of the meeting, the shareholders listened to a presentation that described the terms of the proposed sale. Surprisingly, the shareholders' reaction at the meeting despite the premium price being offered was quite muted. One shareholder stated that he would endorse the sale only as a reflection of the high regard that he had for the company and its management.

There was also an effort by a number of other shareholders to express their deep sadness at seeing the company sold. The affection that these shareholders felt for the company, its employees, and management was clearly evident. Their interests were in long term relationships as well as long term financial returns. The rapid and unexpected decision to sell the company had taken many shareholders by surprise even though they may have recognized this possibility for a number of years. Some of these shareholders probably understood at a very deep level what the sale represented beyond simple dollars and cents.

At the final shareholder's meeting, as well as other meetings and gatherings that followed, there was little opportunity to reflect and mourn the anticipated end of the company's existence as an independent business. The completion of the sale would end the relationship of the current Nelson shareholders and corporate directors, as well as a number of other employees and individuals, with the business. Whatever, the anticipated virtues of the proposed sale, there was a pervasive sadness that was hard to ignore.

Various announcements emphasized the synergies and new opportunities to result from the merger. However, for many employees, the merger meant a time of endings and uncertainties. Some departments and business units anticipated significant changes following the merger, while some employees would soon be leaving the company. For these reasons, a complex array of feelings were simmering just beneath the surface at the various meetings and dinners that followed the announcement of the sale. Part of the problem may have been confusion over whether these meetings were a beginning or an ending -- a celebration of a wedding or a gathering for a wake.

The culture of corporate America does not easily allow for the expression of deep feelings even in a small company like Nelson. These feelings grew out of the many years that the various employees, officers, and shareholders had devoted to the company. They truly felt like they were members of a family -- a family that soon would come to an end. Their ties with the company transcended a simple business relationship.

At Nelson, the shareholders knew the company. They cared about its employees, its products, and its customers. The attitude of these Nelson shareholders was a sharp contrast with that of many investors today who often act on the next earnings report or electronic trade. These investors sometimes buy and sell their stock in a company on little more than idle speculation, a brief news article, or an analyst's passing comment.

In the first week of January, the management and shareholders convened as scheduled to give formal approval to the sale. The meeting was in a small church next to the home office complex in Stoughton. Nelson had recently purchased this building for use as a training center. Very few shareholders attended the meeting since most of them had previously submitted their proxies. The small number seated in the church pews included members of the Board of Directors, some of the senior management, and a scattering of current and former employees. Some of them simply wanted to be present at the end. The atmosphere was quiet and businesslike with more than a passing resemblance to a funeral. Quiet conversation preceded the meeting which took only a few minutes. There was only one question on the agenda. As expected, the shareholders quickly approved the sale of the company.

It is surprisingly easy to bring to an end nearly sixty years of independent corporate history involving the efforts of thousands of individuals. In some ways, the end of a company's independent existence resembles the death of an individual. It seems like something dramatic should happen at such an important event. It doesn't.

On Becoming a Colony

With the sale of Nelson, one of Wisconsin's successful manufacturing firms lost its independence, and the state lost the benefits that accrue from the presence of the headquarters of a significant business. As the new management imposed its own corporate culture and management style, the small company culture and knowledge base that had evolved for nearly 60 years disappeared into a much larger corporation. Much like the loss of a biological species, we can never fully recover the experiences, practices, and procedures that comprised this "organizational DNA."

Unfortunately, the loss of other independent companies with their unique history and culture continues at a rapid rate. Within just a few years following the sale of Nelson, there were a number of other significant corporate mergers that directly affected the Madison area, some of which involved similarly long lived businesses:

- In June of 1998, the Mattel Company announced that it was purchasing the Pleasant Company, a highly successful producer of dolls and related products in Middleton, Wisconsin, just west of Madison.

- A short time later, StarBanc of Cincinnati announced that it was buying Firstar bank of Milwaukee, one of Wisconsin's oldest and largest banks; a few years later, the new Firstar Corporation merged with U.S. Bancorp in Minneapolis to form U.S. Bank.

- In 2000, GE Medical Systems, based in Wisconsin but owned by General Electric in Connecticut, announced that it was purchasing the Lunar Corporation, a Madison producer of medical equipment.

- In August of 2000, a division of Target in Minneapolis announced the purchase of Rowley-Schlimgen, a long time Madison office supply firm.

- The following year, in November of 2001, the Mautz Paint Company, founded in Madison in 1892, announced its acquisition by the Sherwin-Williams Company; in 2002, Sherwin-Williams confirmed, as expected, that it intended to close the Mautz plant in Madison.

- In May of 2002, Sears, Roebuck & Co. announced its plans to purchase Lands' End Inc., a leading Internet retailer with headquarters in Dodgeville, Wisconsin, about 40 miles west of Madison; Lands' End draws many employees from the Madison area and uses a well regarded, small business approach for both its customers and employees.

There are now relatively few firms of substantial size that are headquartered in Madison or even in Wisconsin. When a local firm experiences some degree of success, larger outside corporations often buy it. Out-of-state owners and managers impose their own corporate culture, core values, and management style on these acquired businesses. These new owners increasingly control and direct the future of many Wisconsin businesses. The wealth that they generate flows out of the state to reward distant investors and to support new investments often unrelated to the local business. Wages and state tax revenues decline as high paying executive jobs migrate to distant locations. As a result, Madison and Wisconsin are gradually taking on the characteristics of economic colonies. Outside corporations increasingly control local manufacturing facilities and extract local resources through farming, mining, logging, and drilling for the benefit of absentee owners.

In 2002, *Fortune* magazine again published a list of the 500 largest U.S. corporations. The list illustrates the continued decline of economic power in Wisconsin. It includes 11 companies that have their headquarters in Wisconsin, and only 6 of these 11 companies are members of the top 400. This is incrementally larger than 10 in 1989, but down from 16 in 1979. Comparable states such as Minnesota, Missouri, North Carolina, Virginia, and Washington generally have more and larger businesses on the list with two to three time the combined revenues.

Forbes magazine recently published a similar series of lists that provide separate rankings of companies by their sales, profits, assets, and market value. A state by state comparison reveals similar trends as the *Fortune* compilation. Wisconsin has only about half as many companies on *Forbes'* lists as other fairly comparable states.

One of the reasons for this disparity is that Wisconsin is now home to none of the truly giant corporations listed in the top 100. In fact, many of the great breweries, paper making businesses, and large manufacturing corporations that made Wisconsin their home earlier in the 20th century are no longer on Wisconsin's list. A few large Wisconsin businesses have moved their headquarters out of the state. Some have declared bankruptcy and either vanished or remain in a greatly diminished form. Others have simply not grown rapidly enough to stay in the top 500. However, many Wisconsin companies have lost their independence through purchases by outside corporations. Although there are some exceptions, most companies move the headquarters' functions of acquired companies to their own corporate offices. In this era of continuing mergers, there are a dwindling number of large corporate headquarters in fewer locations. The economic decline of smaller states, such as Wisconsin, will likely spread to larger states as the concentration of economic resources continues.

Our economic system allows the managers and directors of large businesses great latitude in making decisions regarding the future of their corporations. When there is conflict concerning a corporate decision, it is very difficult for individual citizens or local action groups to match the economic and political power of the corporation. In addition, local communities are dependent on the jobs that corporations provide in an era of economic instability. For this reason, local officials are often reluctant to take any action that might cause a loss of jobs.

Nonetheless, despite their concerns, mergers and acquisitions continue with the consequent loss of local jobs, local profits, and local control in communities throughout Wisconsin and elsewhere. In a world of continuing consolidations and concentrations, there is only room for a few big winners. The economies of communities and states lacking the headquarters of significant corporations will become increasingly marginal. Those few communities that are lucky enough to retain the headquarters of surviving corporations will prosper -- until the next merger or corporate decision to move elsewhere also leaves them behind.

The Culture of the Large Corporation

Following a corporate merger, it is not always possible or desirable for employees to adjust to the culture and management of a new and sometimes much larger company. Although every large company is unique, many share some of the cultural characteristics listed in Fig. 1. For example, large organizations typically have a management style featuring a greater number of systems and procedures to control their more complex and extensive operations. Because of these numerous systems and

Small business culture	Large corporate culture
personal style	bureaucratic style
simpler organization	complex organization
coordination easier	coordination more difficult
more relaxed style	more intense style
emphasis on action	emphasis on systems
less structured organization	more formalized procedures
fewer meetings	more meetings
less analysis	more analysis
faster decisions	slower decisions
faster response	slower response
interested in smaller opportunities	focused on larger opportunities
individual impact easier	individual impact harder
smaller number of locations	larger number of locations
management closer	management more distant
to employees, products,	from employees, products,
customers, and shareholders	customers, and shareholders
more local, long term,	more distant, transitory,
informed shareholders	less informed shareholders

Figure 1 - Typical characteristics of business cultures

procedures, managing a larger organization requires a great deal more administrative time and effort than at a smaller company. There are many more meetings and much more travel than at smaller firms, where most of the management team may work within a few minutes of each other. At small companies, lengthy or formal meetings are relatively uncommon. Managers often exchange information through brief, informal meetings or phone conversations. In contrast, larger companies depend on a series of time consuming meetings involving large numbers of attendees.

Large companies also use centralized supporting services for their various units. These centralized groups, often at distant locations, take charge of services in such areas as accounting, personnel, and information systems. As a consequence, local managers find it more difficult to obtain technical or management support or to gain understanding for their specific needs. Smaller, independent companies would typically provide these services at their own local facilities. Using this localized approach, the support is more readily available and highly responsive to the immediate needs of the management.

Managers in large corporations usually emphasize the economies of scale that they believe centralized services can provide. However, the use of centralized services also reflects their preference for a centralized approach to management and control. They often believe that centralized authority is necessary to retain control over widely scattered, disparate activities. It is probably true that smaller firms have less need for centralized approaches to management, since their small size makes communications and control inherently easier. However, highly centralized control is not necessarily the right approach even for larger organizations. As we will see later, these large corporations can benefit from many of the principles of decentralized management often used by small businesses to great advantage.

The extensive number of systems, procedures, and policies in larger organizations creates a need for numerous training sessions. Extensive training sessions, popular in large organizations, demand a great deal of time and can have the ironic effect of deskilling employees. Employees become so busy preparing for and attending training programs that they have less time to do their own jobs. They have less time to use and develop their own skills. They develop a dependency on standardized procedures and policies that gradually come to replace their professional skills and managerial judgment. The net effect can be to create an organization that is less responsive and more bureaucratic.

John Kenneth Galbraith has written of the tendency of managers in modern corporations to delegate their thinking and problem solving to others. However, he may not have recognized that today, corporate managers are often losing their ability to think and solve problems, not to other employees, but to the system itself.

In such a culture, the organization becomes more passive and slower to respond. Managers spend much of their time reacting to requests, rules, and policies made at a distant location. Smaller companies tend to encourage individual initiative and action. This results in a more effective and responsive organization in which the roles and contributions of each employee are clear. As we will see in the following chapters, large organizations could benefit from similar approaches to management.

In smaller organizations, it is easier to maintain a more personal approach to management. Managers can address each situation on an individual basis and consider historical factors, the skills of current employees, and future possibilities in making decisions. What works in one department may not be the best for another. In large organizations, it is more difficult to consider each item or situation on an individual basis. As a result, large corporations can never operate at peak efficiency.

The management culture of the modern, global corporation stresses the need to make objective business decisions based on quantitative analysis unencumbered by tradition or history. However, personal judgment based on experience can inform and guide decisions to avoid making expensive mistakes. Nonetheless, corporate managers and global corporations often minimize the value of the experience of their employees and managers. In fact, these corporations commonly use attractive early retirement packages to encourage their most experienced employees to retire. Managers of, sometimes more fragile, smaller businesses often give greater recognition to the importance of their relatively small number of experienced employees. They understand that the experience of these employees leads to better decisions.

The diverse range of products and locations in a large organization accentuates the management challenges. Organizational linkages can bridge geographical differences. Conversely, a common location can smooth organizational differences. Taken together, the combined functional and geographic differences found within most large organizations make them much more difficult to manage than smaller organizations.

Ongoing corporate mergers create organizations of still greater size and complexity that further accentuate these problems. Issues regarding diverse cultures, product variety, and multiple locations become even more difficult to resolve. In many cases, the term "merger" is simply a euphemism for the corporate purchase or takeover of a smaller firm. The unequal power relationships, compounded in what are sometimes unfriendly takeovers, generate additional challenges. If companies gave more consideration to these issues before deciding to proceed with a merger or business purchase, many of these proposed deals would be less attractive than they first appeared.

Beyond these management considerations, there is a personal dimension to the impact of corporate mergers for the affected employees and their families. Following a corporate sale or merger, employees often find themselves enmeshed in the unfamiliar culture and management style of a large corporation. After doing their jobs with considerable success and effectiveness for many years, they find themselves in new jobs that they had not requested with a new company they had not selected. A multitude of structures, systems, and schedules descends upon them along with an endless cycle of travel, intense meetings, and tight deadlines. Their daily struggles are often frustrating, stressful, and exhausting. As a result, employees often find it more difficult to maintain their personal lives than before the sale.

This is not an uncommon complaint of many employees and managers with high stress jobs in the corporate world that demand long hours, numerous meetings, and substantial travel. They spend their lives responding to endless lists of e-mail messages creating insistent demands for instant action. They often arrive home too late for dinner with their families and regularly work evenings and weekends. International conference calls occur at any time of the day or night. Overseas travel or special assignments often take them away from their homes and family for weeks, months, or even years at a time.

Living such a lifestyle, it is not surprising that people worry about the stability of their marriages and families. Relationships with a spouse or children are difficult to maintain when a job requires such a major commitment of time and energy. Even on those rare occasions when the time is available to be at home or to take a vacation, it is often so brief that it can result in other stresses. A few days of vacation cannot make up for missing months or even years in a relationship.

➢ Summary of effects of corporate mergers

Over the past 20 years, the median wage in Wisconsin has dropped below the national median. Contributing factors likely include the movement of Wisconsin firms to regions that have fewer regulations, still lower wages, and lower taxes; the steady or falling wages of the manufacturing sector; and the declining strength of the labor movement. However, the acquisition of Wisconsin firms by outside corporations with the associated loss of corporate headquarters, higher paying executive jobs, and local accountability has also had a significant impact.

Although the impact of mergers and consolidations has been particularly difficult on many Wisconsin communities, corporate mergers are also profoundly affecting communities in many other states as well as countries throughout the world. Through these mergers, absentee owners are gaining control of local economic resources and exerting a major influence on the economic futures of distant cities, states, and countries. They are making decisions concerning the operation of local facilities, the allocation of costs, the determination of prices, the role of local employees, the use of local suppliers, the production of products, and many other decisions that affect the lives of local residents in a broad variety of ways.

National and global consolidations are reducing the number of centers of economic power. In the United States alone, a relative handful of corporations dominate the production of such products as automobiles, aircraft, petroleum refining, metals, semiconductors, computer software, entertainment, food products, and beverages. A small number of urban centers possess immense concentrations of individual and corporate wealth. Similar and growing concentrations of economic wealth and power are occurring in other countries. As a consequence, many communities in the United States as well as elsewhere are finding that they have decreasing control over their economic future.

In summary, corporate mergers and global capitalism are changing the fundamental relationships between people and their economic livelihood. Some of these changes commonly include:

- the loss of small business culture,

- the imposition of large corporate culture,

- a decrease in economic diversity,

- a decrease in local control over products,

- an increased dependency on outside suppliers,

- a loss of opportunities for local businesses,

- a loss of corporate headquarters,

- a decline in high paying jobs,

- a decline in independent employment opportunities,

- a local wage and benefit structure for remaining jobs driven by the lowest common denominator,

- a decreased tax base,

- a decline in support for the local community, and

- a decline in local control of its economic future.

The following chapters will examine many of these consequences in greater detail. However, there is an important question to consider before those discussions. As we have seen in this chapter, the managers and directors controlling our global corporations exert an overwhelming influence on our lives and society. Their business decisions determine what products companies will produce, who will produce them, as well as where, when, and how. They also determine what their corporations will do with the profits that result from their activities. The next chapter will discuss the source of the power of corporate managers and directors.

Power and the Corporation

The modern auditorium was at the base of a towering skyscraper in the Chicago loop. A large manufacturing corporation that is one of the 100 largest corporations in the country was holding its annual meeting. It had well in excess of 30,000 shareholders, but the total attendance at the annual meeting including various company officers, managers, and employees was barely more than 100 -- about one-third of one percent of the number of shareholders of the corporation. Although several shareholders raised important questions and made significant proposals, there was little substantive discussion or information presented. The entire meeting was a pro-forma ritual virtually devoid of content. It's little wonder that so few shareholders chose to attend.

Clearly, massive corporations have a peripheral relationship with most of their shareholders. Shareholders receive a few written reports that they often do not read and proxy statements that they often do not return. And so, the question arises, "who is making the decisions for these corporations and where do they receive their actual power?"

* * *

The Nature of Corporate Power

• **Directors and shareholders**

Many people, including Peter Drucker, the legendary management consultant, have written at some length attempting to justify the corporate power of directors and senior management. Despite these efforts, there is still not a truly satisfactory explanation of the source of the power of corporate managers and directors or to whom they are accountable. As a result, the growing power wielded by corporate management is disturbing to many thoughtful individuals.

For example, today's corporations generally do not use an inclusive process to solicit input from their affected constituencies when making important business decisions such as mergers. Corporate boards invariably make these types of decisions behind tightly closed doors. Although the directors of a corporation often mention their responsibilities to multiple constituencies, in reality, they represent the interests of the shareholders of the company above the interests of all other constituencies.

Furthermore, even shareholder representation is surprisingly weak and indirect. Although the shareholders nominally elect the directors, as shown in Fig. 2, in reality the system is not as open as is sometimes claimed and is often self-perpetuating. The board selects the chief executive officer (CEO) who, in turn, commonly suggests candidates for nomination as new or continuing directors. The new directors are often friends or acquaintances of the CEO. Experience has shown that they are not likely to seriously question the actions of the CEO except under the most extraordinary situations. Even then, the board is often slow to respond.

In a similar way, the directors elect the other officers of the company, although the CEO typically does the actual selection and hiring. And so, the officers, as both employees and officers of the corporation, have a divided responsibility to both the CEO and the directors.

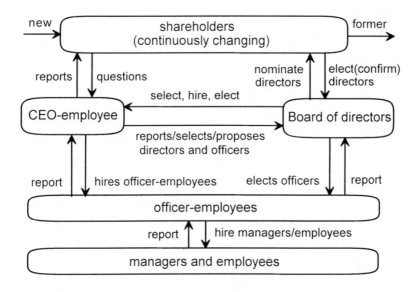

Figure 2 - Power flows in corporations

Despite efforts to diversify the composition of their boards, some corporations also still retain directors with either current or former ties to the company or special relationships with the CEO. This can include former employees as well as friends from other companies or the government. These directors often fail to have the independence that their jobs require. Multiple, cross-linked board memberships with different companies further concentrate corporate power in the hands of a small number of senior executives and directors.

Following nominations made by the board, the vote of the shareholders for corporate directors is often a formality. In large, publicly traded companies, there are many shareholders with little detailed knowledge of the firm, and elections are even less likely to be meaningful than in smaller companies. These shareholders rarely visit the firms that they own or attend the annual meetings of the corporation. Their ownership is usually transitory. They may sell their stock on short notice for almost any reason. They simply observe the proceedings from a distance with little influence or long term interest in the company. The typical corporate rhetoric that the shareholders own the business and elect a board to represent them in the running of the business is more fiction than reality for most large corporations.

In the 1980s and 1990s, the investment community, recognizing the validity of many of these observation, began to encourage corporations to create a greater distance between the board and the company's management. They also attempted to ensure better representation of the shareholders' interests by encouraging directors to own company stock and by tying executive compensation to stock valuations through the use of performance bonuses and stock options. Directors also adopted measures to discourage hostile takeovers of their companies.

What has been the effect of these changes in corporate governance? Executives have learned how to manage their companies earnings in such a way as to meet Wall Street's expectations, trigger their bonuses, and enhance the value of their options. Corporate organizational and financial structures have become ever more complex as executives continue to search for new ways to report increased corporate earnings. Shareholders see short-lived rises in the stock price followed by sharp declines as the manipulations encouraged by this new style of corporate management become apparent. Yet, despite all the changes, the distance between the typical global corporation and its shareholders, not to mention its local communities, remains large.

For these reasons, the decisions that large corporations make concerning whether to close a plant, purchase a company, or sell the firm usually reflect the views of a small group of board members, executives, and investors. Their accountability to their shareholders, employees, and communities is relatively weak. Short term financial considerations often dominate their decisions. Such decisions may not be in the best long term interests of employees, local communities, other constituencies, or even many shareholders.

Some of these decisions, such as closing a manufacturing plant or dropping a product line, primarily affect a specific group of workers and their community. Other decisions, such as restructuring, selling, or merging the company can have much more far reaching effects. One of these is the impact of the change in the location of the corporate headquarters.

• The benefits of corporate headquarters

Many people fail to recognize the importance of the location of the corporate headquarters for a community. Instead, they focus their attention on the number of jobs involved in any corporate decision to relocate facilities. Since corporate headquarters often do not involve as many jobs as a large manufacturing plant, the impact of a change in its location may seem relatively insignificant.

This perspective fails to recognize the disproportionate importance of the headquarters location for most companies. Managers make important corporate decisions at the headquarters location. Remote ownership reduces access to these high level decision makers. It is more difficult for senior managers to consider local concerns in their decisions. Following a merger, the new owners usually reduce the number of senior positions at the local facility. Corporate profits flow to the headquarters community. Most of the highly compensated managerial and professional employees work at the home office. It is less likely that that there will be further expansions in the local community or new facilities in the surrounding area.

Centralized control from a distant corporate headquarters often imposes costs on local business units that are not necessary for the operation of that unit. These may include additional travel, meetings, reviews, reports, administrative expenses, personal costs, and so on. The future success of the local unit becomes more uncertain.

Corporations often apply decisions made at distant locations throughout the organization even when business problems unrelated to the local facility may be responsible. Restructuring plans often include uniform employment reductions at all units of the company even though their relative contributions to the company's problems are usually quite different. Thus, local units that become part of larger corporations can suffer the consequences of business problems to which they did not contribute or that they could not control.

The local community finds it more difficult to find people with the time, skills, and community knowledge to serve as directors of local nonprofit groups. Support for local civic improvements decreases as resources flow to the location of the corporate headquarters. As we have seen throughout history, resources tend to flow away from colonies to the centers of power.

Similar problems exist on a much larger scale throughout the world. The theory of comparative advantage suggests that with free trade and open markets each participant will gravitate toward producing that which it can produce most efficiently, even on a relative basis. That is, even if there are no goods or services for which an individual, company, or the country is the most efficient, they will still produce those goods or services for which they are relatively most efficient. This will allow the most efficient producer to shift their resources into areas where their comparative advantage is the greatest. There is greater overall production of goods and services.

Driven by the demands for short term profits, there is a tendency for the decisions of absentee managers to undermine the strengths of free trade and the concept of comparative advantage. Foreign ownership of a country's productive resources can result in a decision to halt production at local plants if they are less efficient than facilities in other countries. Thus, absentee owners can abandon the productive capacity and labor force of entire countries.

A recent article on the failing economy and rising unemployment in Argentina noted the closing of older, less productive facilities owned by foreign corporations. Without much publicity, the global economy has set aside the theory of comparative advantage used for years to justify decreasing trade barriers and to encourage free trade. A new principle of absolute advantage is replacing the classic concept of comparative advantage. There is no place for any individual, plant, or country unless it is as efficient as the most productive unit in the world. Given this impossible standard, it is not surprising that the amount of economic dislocation and suffering is on the rise.

The Technological Underground

• The control of nature

In addition to their physical distance from local communities, many corporate executives and directors of large corporations are relatively isolated from its actual products and functions. They often work in a sort of closed environment comprised mainly of others like themselves. They are many levels removed from the workers who perform the physical tasks necessary to sustain the company.

The synthetic world of corporate management is part of the physical and metaphorical underground described by Rosalind Williams in her book, *Notes on the Underground.* Williams discusses the modern world using a metaphor based on the underground infrastructure constructed in our cities during the nineteenth century for subways and sewers. The emerging technological society resembles an underground world of artificial environments separated from the natural world that exists on the surface.

Beneath the synthetic underground exists a "deep underground" that is out of sight for most people. It is the metaphorical equivalent of the boiler room of a building -- essential, but unseen. The deep underground is where workers produce the raw materials, food, and finished products that sustain the artificial world of the technological underground. It includes the "dirty" parts of industrial society such as open pit mines, chemical plants, steel mills, large scale agriculture, food processing plants, and assembly lines.

Other writers have used similar language. Anais Nin in her novelette, *The Voice,* describes a region beneath the normal reach of elevators where one finds darkness and necessary, but unpleasant, aspects of life such as tombs and prisons. John Updike in the opening pages of his novel, *Rabbit is Rich,* writes of mechanics emerging from the dark underworld beneath the hood of a car. Octavio Paz in his book of essays, *The Other Voice,* even describes poets as miners toiling under the offices of the large publishing houses.

Figure 3 presents a more complete model using the metaphor of the underground. The deeper levels of the

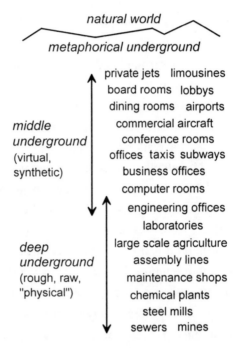

Figure 3 - Underground as metaphor for corporation

underground contain the physical activities related to the delivery of goods and services. Engineers and technicians working in laboratories develop the materials and products used in the upper levels of the underground. Assembly line workers manufacture these products in factories often in a distant city or country. Maintenance workers perform the essential services required to keep the underground operating. Just like the boiler room deep in the sub-basement of a large office building, these facilities, factories, and workers are virtually invisible to most corporate employees. The deep underground of noise, dirt, and danger is a world apart from the polished chrome, wood paneling, and thick carpet of the corporate office building.

Despite their different focus and location, the deeper levels of the underground and the natural surface are bound together by their intense connection to the physical world. The natural world of forests and prairies is much different than the technological world of factories and laboratories, but they both fully engage our senses, respond to physical laws, and are difficult to control.

Nonetheless, in order to meet the demands of the market for predictable results, corporate managers attempt to impose as much control as possible over their operations. The world of nature exists as a distinct and independent entity that is a continual threat to corporate control. Many corporations attempt to subdue nature in a variety of ways. They level forests. They plant grass and pave the land. They surround their facilities with walls and fences. They secure, seal, and air condition their buildings to create controlled environments.

Many corporate managers and executives spend much of their time in the upper levels of the underground surrounded by the synthetic and artificial. It is a world designed to eliminate any harsh intrusions on their senses -- a metaphorical underground of airport terminals, airplanes, and conference rooms. They often spend their days traveling to meetings and answering phone calls and e-mail messages. They rarely touch a product, visit a factory, or see a laboratory. In fact, many corporations simply focus on financial trading and speculation removing their managers even further from the physical world.

Corporations extend their world vertically through the creation of a metaphorical underground of towering skyscrapers served by vertical subways of elevators and connected by long hallways and tunnels. Automobiles, trains, and planes travel a virtual subway system of limited access expressways, high speed railways, and controlled flight corridors. The corporate employee can literally spend days traveling around the world without leaving the virtual underground.

Nonetheless, in the final analysis, corporations find that they cannot completely control nature. Nature asserts its power through devastating storms, earthquakes, droughts, and other natural disasters. Long term climatic and geological phenomena produce inevitable and uncontrollable change. Despite the best efforts of corporations to shape nature to their service, nature remains an independent force that threatens their control. It has existed for eons before the creation of corporations and the virtual underground. It bends, but refuses to break, when corporate power tries to destroy it. Thus, it threatens the ability of the corporation to produce the predictable results that the market demands.

More profoundly, the power of nature not only threatens the power of the corporation, but it challenges the underlying corporate values. It provides an alternate world view to that of global capitalism and the global corporation -- it serves as an independent moral reference frame. Rather than responding to the short term demands of the corporation for productivity or efficiency, nature pursues a strategy based on long term survival. Natural processes teach us the characteristics of long lived systems. They emphasize the interconnected nature of life. They demonstrate the importance of a diversity of species. They depend on a clean environment. Despite the efforts of some to create a synthetic world under their control, we all remain part of nature and subject to its processes and constraints. Through this realization, we gain a sense of humility regarding our own importance and vulnerability.

• The control of time

In addition to nature, time represents another aspect of reality that the corporation cannot control. In the recent novel by Michael Crichton, *Timeline*, one of the characters describes the inability of the corporation to shape or control the past. The past stands aloof from the goals and desires of the modern corporation. History has often represented a threat to the established power structure. For this reason, much of our conventional history, written from the perspective of the winners, fails to include alternative perspectives and experiences. Along with nature, it represents an independent threat to the omnipotence of the corporation. This may be one of the reasons that corporate management so often devalues the past. It challenges the actions of the corporation through the experiences of past generations.

Although corporations, as with our greater society, may try to change our knowledge of the past by suppressing or rewriting history, it is difficult, if not impossible to permanently hide these realities. The organizational memory is often hard to erase. Employees remember the past and can challenge attempts to revise it. This may help explain why corporations following a merger often encourage experienced workers to leave through early retirement packages, generous severance packages, or other means.

Just as the past poses a potential threat to the power and control of the modern corporation, the future represents a threat to the stability and survival of the virtual world created by the corporation. The future represents life, death, and renewal. Despite all of our collective efforts at denial, we are unable to refute these fundamental realities. People die, buildings decay, new products become obsolete, successful businesses weaken and ultimately close. At the same time, new people are born, society changes, ideas evolve, new forces emerge, technology changes, competition emerges. Thus, the corporation does not want to look too far into the future. The future is the great unknown looming on the horizon that resists control.

As a result of these combined threats from both the past and the future, the modern, global corporation often tends to devalue the past, ignore the future, and focus its concerns only on the vanishing present. It is in the present where the corporation tries to use its power to maximum effect. Employees spend their days in a frantic flurry of activity focused on the rapidly changing, ever elusive present.

While riding in a jet aircraft or even a high speed car or train, our focus in time and space often seems to shrink to the moment and the space we are experiencing. At high speeds, the past recedes quickly and is of little interest. Pilots of high performance aircraft and drivers of racing cars ignore all but the immediate future in light of the demands of the present as they negotiate each turn and maneuver as quickly and accurately as possible. In much the same way, the demands of global capitalism discourage any efforts to reflect on the past or to consider the future in light of persistent and intense demands for maximum returns in the present.

Frantic activity can be quite addictive. Many of us associate speed and action with growth and progress. When we slow down and take a much-needed vacation, we feel like we are missing something. It takes a long time to realize that there are different ways to grow and that progress can require slowing down. Sometimes we have to step off the train to get where we want to go.

Stewart Brand, in his recent book, *The Clock of the Long Now,* discusses his efforts to expand our view of time and space. He derived the title of his book from the common phrase, "the here and now." In a chapter titled "The Long Now," he quotes Brian Eno concerning our changing views of "here" and "now." They both note that for many of us "here" is continuing to get smaller until for some people it might be simply their own personal living space. Some recent commercials even seem to suggest that "here" can be as small as the inside of an automobile or airplane.

In the same way, "now" is also shrinking. Brand and Eno suggest that for many of us "now" describes a period of about a week. For some commercials, the "now" in our culture of instant gratification can be as short as a brief moment in time. As an alternative, Brand quotes a passage by Eno that suggests consideration of "the big here and the long now," out of which grew the title of Brand's book. Such a perspective would encourage us to view our actions and inactions in terms of both their impact throughout the world and on future generations.

Many smaller, often privately owned, businesses take the long term perspective in their business decisions. Nelson supported the development of active sound control technology and Digisonix. In another example, a recent article described New Balance Athletic Shoe, a privately owned domestic manufacturer of athletic shoes. New Balance is reportedly the last company in the industry still manufacturing shoes in the

United States. According to the article, it has been able to maintain its domestic manufacturing through investments in technology, teamwork among its workers, and, perhaps most importantly, a long term investment perspective. Its private ownership enables New Balance to focus on the development of its business over the long haul rather than meeting investor demands for immediate profits.

In today's world of the short now, many large corporations not only make their decisions based on short term results, but they also consider only economic criteria in their decision making processes. They have a reluctance to give in-depth consideration to the non-economic dimensions of a problem. Unfortunately, our society often applies this same short term, economic perspective to decisions made by other institutions including our schools, churches, and government.

We sometimes forget that there are other more expansive views of time and space that have proven to be effective. For example, the Christian church values the past, takes a very long term perspective, and has a global view of its mission. Despite the continuing conflicts related to its diverse views on social and moral issues, it has survived and prospered for two thousand years. Nonetheless, in today's world, even church administrators follow the latest business fads with enthusiasm and fail to recognize the inherent strengths of their own core values, traditions, and theology.

A sharp contrast with the high speed world of airplanes or global capitalism exists in the world of medicine. Physicians often tell patients recovering from a wide range of illnesses or injuries to rest or moderate their activity level and to slow down. As we rest and relax, we often begin to recall memories from our past. We begin to consider our lives in the context of the future. We rediscover or strengthen our relationships. Much like a tree with a broken branch, healing and growth often begin when there is time and space available.

• The control of image

In addition to creating a synthetic physical world which they believe that they can control, corporations also attempt to control their corporate image. In fact, they can appear more concerned with their image than the physical reality behind the image. Moving beyond the fancy corporate office buildings, we find corporate activities contributing to air, water, and noise pollution. Large corporations often resist efforts by the government to control this pollution and to cleanup the aftermath of earlier spills and contamination for economic reasons. As a result, society must bear the costs of this pollution through its impact on our collective health, the quality of our lives, and the costs of remediation.

On the aesthetic level, endless shopping plazas with "big box" stores owned and operated by large corporations dominate the urban landscape in many communities. The almost endless, sun baked, asphalt parking lots in front of these massive buildings are often unbroken even by islands for pedestrians, trees, grass, or flower beds.

In some communities, there are regulations that require a certain amount of landscaping to break up the impact of large parking lots. In others, the size and design of signs are regulated as well. These are small things that improve the environment and do not cost a great deal of money, but in our hyper competitive world, many businesses will make these investments only if they must comply with regulations.

Similarly, some global corporations make token contributions to local community projects while most of their profits and wealth flow out of the community. Nonetheless, these modest initiatives are regularly the subject of highly publicized "news" events and sometimes featured in commercials. In yet another area, stores emphasize their "buy America" programs by reporting small initiatives with American suppliers while they fill their stores with foreign goods from literally dozens of different countries sometimes produced under questionable conditions.

Despite the great lengths to which many corporations go to control their physical world and their corporate image, they often don't seem to have as much concern about their residual impact when they leave a community or discontinue operations. We still have problems and disputes regarding who will pay the immense costs of cleaning up the environmental impact of many business activities. In Wisconsin, long lasting chemicals from discontinued manufacturing or paper making practices pollute Lake Michigan as well as many rivers and render the fish potentially dangerous to eat. Many states have similar problems with the effects of mining wastes leftover from long closed mines.

Other residual effects may be less infamous, but can still be quite troubling in their own way. Intense competition between large stores results in huge buildings and parking lots that companies often abandon when they don't meet expected profitability levels. As a result, the community has a vacant eyesore in its midst. The city of Sturgeon Bay, in Wisconsin's

Door County, recently found itself with such a vacant property when a discount store decided to close its doors. The facility and parking lot are so large that alternative uses for the property have been difficult to identify. It has remained vacant for a number of years.

Ironically, while pondering the future of this vacant facility, Sturgeon Bay was also debating the location of a new traffic signal that a large retail chain requested as a condition to building a new store in the city. Despite the feelings of some that the requested location was not optimum for overall traffic flow, the community was reluctant to lose the new store. Some residents emphasized that the store would increase the tax base, provide additional shopping alternatives, and attract further residential and commercial expansion. Others expressed concern that the area was already short of workers during the busy summer tourism season.

Besides the traffic signal, the store requested variances in the size and placement of its sign as well as exceptions to setback and landscaping related requirements. It hoped to obtain a state grant to cover about three-fourths of the cost of sewer, water, and street improvements. The company also reportedly needed a permit due to a wetland on the proposed site. Meanwhile, despite the public costs and environmental impact of these plans, the large building that formerly housed the previous discount store remained empty.

Amazingly, about the same time that the new retail chain made this proposal to enter the Sturgeon Bay market, the owners of an existing large discount store submitted a plan to the city for a new and much larger store as well. City officials responded with a variety of appropriate questions on the impact of yet another major building and expressed concern over the future of their existing store. They presumably don't want to end up with two large, vacant buildings in their community as well as two new, even larger buildings whose ultimate future may also be uncertain.

Externalized Costs and the Local Community

In addition to their negative impact on the aesthetic environment, large stores often cause additional damage to the economic fabric of the community by taking substantial business from the small family owned businesses in the traditional downtown business district. Large stores have repeated this pattern in many small communities throughout the United States. Nonetheless, many communities continue to court and encourage large mega-stores due to the presumed benefits of economic development.

However, large scale businesses bring costs as well as benefits, and communities do not always appreciate the way in which retail mega-stores and large corporations are able to transfer many of these costs to the local community. The price tags for their products or services do not include these externalized costs, but ultimately we all pay for them. These transferred costs help these companies increase their reported profits in an economy that places perceived productivity and efficiency above all other considerations.

Typical examples of direct and indirect costs that large stores and other corporations often impose on the community include:

- the construction of new roads serving their businesses;

- the impact of increased traffic on the community;

- the environmental impacts of facilities and processes;
- the improvement of utilities and support services;
- the public support of training programs;
- the impact of large employment fluctuations;
- the impact of seasonal and temporary employees;
- the loss of locally-owned retailers and suppliers;
- the loss of a customer base for remaining suppliers;
- the loss of variety in shopping and employment opportunities; and
- the impact of vacated buildings and facilities.

A recent proposal to build a large mega-store in Fort Atkinson, Wisconsin, provides a good example of some of these problems. However, in a somewhat surprising turn of events that may become more common, this proposal has come under considerable scrutiny precisely due to the costs that will result from the project for the local community.

The proposed location is a site that is substantially beyond the area currently served by city water and sewer. The new store would require the city to provide these services much sooner than anticipated to an area some distance from the existing downtown. In addition, the city recently upgraded this downtown district at considerable cost. The owner of the proposed store has reportedly offered to provide about 25% of these expenses, but this means that the city will still have to provide about 75% of the costs for developments that are otherwise unneeded at the present time. Due to concerns from city officials over these additional costs as well as opposition to the project from some residents, consideration of the proposed project is proceeding slowly. Other communities would benefit from a similar careful analysis of requests for development of outlying areas.

In addition to costs transferred to the general community, corporations can also transfer many other costs to customers, employees, suppliers, and other institutions. They may use automated telephone systems to eliminate customer service employees at the expense of their customers. They may negotiate direct reductions of costs such as the benefits and wages of employees. They may also avoid the costs of additional benefits by demanding that their current employees work overtime instead of hiring additional employees.

Seasonal, temporary, and contract workers are examples of cost externalization in which the corporation avoids the expenses associated with providing year-round employment. Although the use of seasonal workers is perhaps unavoidable in some businesses, in other businesses it is optional. Some manufacturing firms, including Nelson in the early 1980s, try to avoid layoffs during times when business is slow in order to retain their skilled work force. Some home contractors do their best to provide employment through their seasonally slower winter months for the same reason.

Unfortunately, temporary or seasonal work is still quite common. These seasonal workers must find or the community must provide economic support during the remainder of the year. In the past, migrant workers were the most common example of this form of employment, and it became well known for its inadequate pay, lack of benefits, transitory lifestyle, and uncertain income. Sadly, we routinely accept variations of this form of employment throughout our economy today without much debate, much as we accept the acquisition of local businesses, loss of local control, and transfer of valuable jobs without much protest.

Manufacturing firms externalize costs through the use of subcontractors that have lower wage scales, fewer benefits, or poorer working conditions. They may transfer additional costs, associated with activities such as inspection, warehousing, and transportation, to their suppliers through the use of mandated product quality standards such as ISO 9000 and just-in-time (JIT) delivery systems. In some businesses, such as the health care industry, they may solicit volunteers who will actually work for free.

Despite the great success that corporations have had in transferring their direct and indirect costs to others, some people think this does not go far enough. They are working hard to have corporations actually compensated while imposing their costs on others. For many years, some conservative politicians and business leaders have supported the "takings" concept which asks that society compensate corporations for any governmental action which reduces their profits. Through this concept, supposedly justified by constitutional restraints against the taking of property without proper compensation, business advocates propose that corporations receive compensation for the financial impact of new environmental laws. Of course, this perspective conveniently overlooks the negative impact of polluted air, contaminated water, and global climate changes on the property rights of others.

Although environmentalists successfully fought the concept in Congress by noting that it was simply an effort to pay polluters not to pollute, it continues to be a problem on the international level. Under the North American Free Trade Agreement (NAFTA), foreign investors in the United States, Canada, or Mexico are able to sue these governments for the loss of profits due to pollution control legislation. Recently, new proposals modeled on NAFTA for a Free Trade Area of the Americas (FTAA) may expand similar corporate rights throughout the western hemisphere.

The net effect of these provisions is to discourage governmental action to improve environmental protection. Although this is a problem for the United States, it would have even more severe consequences in countries whose environmental laws lag U.S. standards. Beyond the impact of these trade agreements on environmental protection, there is also speculation that they will contain provisions that may further strengthen the power of global corporations over the use and control of technology.

The dominance of the corporate business paradigm is so strong that we can even see its influence in our non-business institutions. For example, a significant segment of our society demands that students improve their performance on various standardized tests. For some, the one-dimensional score on a test has the allure of a simple, quantitative measure of education. It parallels the way in which the one-dimensional determination of profit provides a simple, if inadequate, measure of corporate performance.

In response, many schools have increased the amount of homework that they assign to their students. However, this expanded use of homework provides another, though perhaps unintentional, example of cost externalization. Restricted in their ability to hire additional teachers and reduce class size in an era that resists increased educational expenditures, schools effectively enlist parents, whether or not qualified, to serve as unpaid teaching assistants both at home and in the schools.

Similarly, difficulties in obtaining additional state budget support have encouraged a number of public sector institutions, including state universities, to externalize more of their costs. One way in which universities have done this is to expand the range of services that they offer to commercial and industrial firms.

The "Wisconsin idea" encompasses a vision of seeing the boundaries of the university as extending to the boundaries of the state. This progressive perspective has long encouraged the application of university knowledge to provide benefits throughout the state. However, in Wisconsin as well as other states, financial pressures have led to an expansion and commercialization of these activities to an extent that may threaten the fundamental educational and research missions of the university. For this reason, we need to reexamine university-industry partnerships in such areas as joint research projects, entrepreneurial activities, and consulting assignments.

In many cases, these services are directly competitive with small, privately owned businesses such as consulting firms, training institutes, and technical laboratories. Due to their public support and tax advantages, universities are able to offer their services for a price that these private businesses find difficult to match. This is possible because public and quasi-public organizations have many streams of revenue to cover their overall costs, and because these organizations usually do not need to generate a direct return on the public's investment.

University professors offer consulting services to corporations without the need to cover the costs of their infrastructure since their universities already provide this infrastructure to them at no cost. Universities also make their facilities available for private use at a fee that does not necessarily need to cover all costs since the facility is already available. In some cases, corporations are able to avoid payment of overhead charges to the university for sponsored research through the use of gifts or grants. In addition, corporations are able to receive the benefits of university research projects that are heavily dependent upon graduate students who receive a small fraction of the salaries paid to their counterparts in private sector research laboratories.

Corporate business leaders typically praise these various commercial activities of our universities and other public sector institutions as a way to provide additional funding and reduce dependency on taxes while increasing accountability. However, in most cases, the universities and other institutions remain heavily tax-subsidized and the increased accountability is primarily to the corporations that are partners in these efforts. As a result, large corporations achieve considerable influence over public sector activities as well as the benefits of services subsidized by public expenditures.

All of the examples in this section demonstrate that one of the easiest ways to improve the productivity of a paid labor force is to have others, paid less or not at all, take on their tasks. Mark Twain described the basic business principle in *Tom Sawyer* when Tom had others pay him to white wash his fence. It seems that global corporations are now practicing their own version to near perfection. It is entirely possible that cost externalization has had at least as much to do with recent corporate cost reductions as the application of new technologies or so-called efficiency measures.

We need to develop new approaches to our societal decisions that include more explicit consideration of these various externalized costs. We also need to do a better job of identifying the sources of corporate power and ensuring greater accountability of those making corporate decisions. Society created the corporate form of business organization to better meet its needs. In exchange for the products and services that they provide, society granted corporations a variety of special privileges. For these reasons, corporations should have a mission and set of values that goes beyond financial returns for the shareholders. The benefits of incorporation should carry with them a more balanced set of obligations to the overall community.

Decline of Economic Diversity

In the 1950s, tiny corner grocery stores dotted the neighborhoods of many cities. Young children could walk down the street to buy groceries, ice cream, or candy. Larger stores on main street were open late on Friday nights. Even in smaller cities, the shopping district might include department stores, grocery stores, bakeries, jewelry stores, clothing stores, dime stores, movie theaters, pharmacies, diners, and banks, often owned and operated by local shopkeepers.

Today, intense competition from huge shopping malls dominated by national chain stores and mega-stores has decimated these main street shopping districts. In fact, some discount stores offer most of main street's products and services in a single building. However, despite their size, these stores cannot duplicate the personal services, connections to the community, and stability provided by main street stores. The overall economic diversity of our communities has decreased, and with it, the richness of our lives.

* * *

The Value of Economic Diversity

Diversity is a powerful concept that provides many advantages for our environment, organizations, and society. A diversity of species in an ecosystem provides sustainability and stability. A diversity of individuals in an organization brings a wider range of knowledge and experiences.

A diversity of ideas in a meeting often results in better solutions. Our society also benefits from economic diversity. Economic diversity grows with an increase in the number, location, and variety of businesses, distribution channels, purchasing options, employment opportunities, management styles, business cultures, and so on. As with ecological diversity, there are many factors that can reduce economic diversity and increase economic risk. These include business closings, mergers, and reorganizations as well as standardized management practices and standards.

The senior Nelson managers were a diverse group with a variety of management styles. Nelson's various units reflected these differences. The Nelson management allowed each business unit to develop its own unique subculture which provided the company with considerable business diversity for its relatively small size.

Despite some similarities in their product lines, the Nelson and Universal Silencer units of Nelson Industries operated with substantial autonomy, each developing a distinctive style and culture that reflected the needs and personalities of their managers and customers. Nelson's management gave its smaller units similar freedom to develop their own business approaches. Digisonix created a subculture appropriate for its high technology business. Professional Data Processing (PDP) created a subculture to meet the unique needs of its computer services business. The Nelson corporate group developed a distinctive subculture based on its broad view of the company.

As a private corporation, Nelson's quarterly operating results did not dominate management's actions to the same extent as in many larger, public corporations. Nelson's managers could more readily make decisions based on the long term needs of the various business units while recognizing that each unit played a different role within the overall corporation. As the economy went through its normal cycles, each of the various units of the company would find itself at a different point in its own business cycle. These differences often helped offset fluctuations in the overall economic cycle.

The industrial silencer business depended on large capital expenditures by its customers for plants and equipment that tended to lag the overall economic cycle. The muffler and filter businesses were dependent on purchases of mobile equipment and vehicles that responded more quickly to current economic conditions. Digisonix had long term development contracts that brought in significant revenue even while the overall economy was slowing in the early 1990s.

Following corporate mergers or sales, the cultures of acquired businesses often begin to change. Reorganizations, consolidations of smaller units, and the imposition of more standardized procedures and centralized controls create greater cultural uniformity.

Integrating business units, centralizing services, and standardizing business practices may provide some short term efficiencies, but these savings come with a long term price. There is less flexibility in evaluating new business ideas or novel technologies. There is a loss of specialized knowledge that evolves in each subculture. There are fewer opportunities for management training and development. There are fewer options when problems arise. The company is more vulnerable to the effects of the business cycle. For these reasons, there is more value than many managers recognize in retaining independent smaller units within a large organization.

Agriculture provides a good example of the value of economic diversity to our local communities and overall society. Family farms produce a highly diverse range of products that are available at local markets on a regular basis. They have a personal connection to the land and local community that is responsive to local needs. As local, independent food producers, they are more resistant to disruptions due to transportation or other factors. They purchase many of their supplies and materials at the local level. Their owners support and attend local churches, schools, and community activities.

Large corporate farms typically have a narrow focus on productivity that they pursue by constructing huge facilities to produce a single product. They invest in expensive equipment and facilities often purchased from large, distant suppliers that reduce their relative need for employees. Nonetheless, there is considerable evidence that these large scale facilities do not necessarily have greater efficiency even when things work as planned.

When things don't work as planned, they can cause significant problems. Although engineers often design large farms using advanced environmental protection schemes, natural disasters can overwhelm these protections. Several years ago, a hurricane in North Carolina resulted in the flooding of a number of facilities housing large numbers of animals and created an environmental disaster. Smaller farms distributed over a much larger area tend to limit the total damage that a single storm can produce.

Concentration of production facilities can create other problems. The loss of a single large facility due to natural, technological, or economic disaster can have a major impact on the regional or even national economy. A small number of suppliers now produce many critical electronic components and products for the world's economy. A few years ago, an earthquake in Taiwan affected the sale of high technology products worldwide due to the loss of memory chips from production facilities in the affected area.

Thoughtful persons have expressed similar concerns with an agricultural system increasingly dominated by a small number of large corporations. However, in these cases, it is our food supply that is at risk rather than simply the latest electronic consumer item. The recent destruction of many farm herds in Europe due to hoof and mouth disease and mad cow disease is a good demonstration of the dangers of agricultural and economic concentrations.

Mergers and the Loss of Diversity

In addition to contributing to a world economy that is less stable, and ultimately less sustainable, the loss of economic diversity due to mergers and the growth of mega-businesses can result in other problems for individuals, local communities, and even national governments. From an employment perspective, mergers reduce the number of independent employers. The quarterly results of a single large corporation have a profound impact on local hiring decisions at many different locations. Overall, the health of a single company strongly affects the economic health of many local communities.

With fewer independent companies, there are fewer customers for other suppliers to sell their goods and services. In relatively decentralized smaller companies, the various business units operate in a semi-autonomous manner and often make their own purchasing decisions. After a merger with a larger company, reorganizations or eliminations of these units can produce a disproportionate reduction in business opportunities for other suppliers in the local community. Rather than simply losing a single firm, the local economy loses the impact of multiple semi-independent business units.

Ironically, corporate mergers often also create major problems for the merging corporations. The costs and complexities of reconciling two different systems for accounting, marketing, and production can be much larger than anticipated. Different computer hardware and software as well as contrasting corporate cultures further compound the problems. The new, larger organization is more unwieldy and coordination throughout the organization becomes more inefficient. Rather than producing the synergistic savings promoted to gain support for a proposed merger, a merger can result in a new organization that is less able to serve the customer base of the two merging organizations.

However, despite an often flawed premise, the problems of corporations are at least due to their own decisions. The problems experienced by individuals and communities as a result of a merger, such as personnel reductions, are not due to their decisions. Nonetheless, they still must deal with must deal with the aftermath of these economic dislocations. Mergers and consolidations lead to a world with a few big winners and many others who are struggling to maintain their current economic position. Members of an increasingly desperate underclass find it difficult to support themselves with full time jobs paying minimal wages.

At the same time, even in countries like the United States where there are still substantial regulations despite the impact of deregulation efforts, economic consolidations are reducing the ability of the government to control economic activity. In response to proposed legislation or regulations that may restrict their businesses, corporations sometimes move or threaten to move their businesses to those states or countries where labor is cheaper, environmental controls are less restrictive, or there is less government interference. For example, recent opposition to sales taxes on Internet purchases has focused on the ability of Internet companies to avoid these taxes by moving overseas.

In addition to the economic effects, there are other non-economic problems with corporate mergers and consolidations. For example, five giant companies dominate the music recording industry and exert considerable control over the recording and distribution of music throughout the world. As a result, a relatively small number of individuals have a disproportionate influence over the direction of our recorded music. Society loses the cultural diversity and richness of choices that an industry with a larger and more diverse group of companies could provide.

These companies often own the master recordings for their music. Although the copyrights on recordings have a finite lifetime, the world's access to this music is dependent on the stability and willingness of a few companies to protect and make available the master recordings. Similar problems exist related to the cost and accessibility of movies, video recordings, and books. Ephemeral electronic media and downloads from the Internet are further increasing the importance of the continuing presence of a corporate supplier. Although individuals may retain individual copies of some downloaded material, they usually do not have rights to distribute this material and may be difficult to locate.

Such problems go beyond the content of specific works. Henry Jenkins, in a recent commentary, expressed concern over the impact of corporate ownership and control of the many fictional characters that are part of our collective cultural history. Global corporations increasingly create and own rights to our cultural icons. Such diverse authors as David Maybury-Lewis and Murray Gell-Mann have discussed the importance of cultural diversity for a healthy society. Today, our cultural diversity continues to decrease as our global society becomes ever more privatized and homogenized.

Large corporations also dominate ownership of other media businesses. This dominance threatens editorial diversity, independence, accessibility, and prices. For example, a few huge corporations now own most of our major television networks and ownership of individual stations and cable systems by a single group is increasing. Unfortunately, several recent court decisions rejected proposed rules that would have placed restrictions on such purchases. It appears that it will be difficult to control further consolidations in these industries without new legislative regulatory authority.

Similar problems exist in radio broadcasting. The Telecommunications Act of 1996 allowed businesses to own up to 6-8 radio stations in a given market with no limit on the overall total. In Madison, this has resulted in six radio stations, including one of the leading news stations, being owned by a company that owns over 1100 radio stations nationwide as well as its own radio network. Such consolidations raise concern over the direction of the political and musical content of the programming on these stations.

The problems of consolidation also extend to the print media. Although Madison is a notable exception, even most large cities today have only a single newspaper often owned by an outside corporation. Similarly, large multinational corporations control a growing portion of the book publishing and distribution industry. Soaring prices for scientific journals, published by a declining number of large publishers, are a major problem for many research libraries.

An Ecological View of Diversity

• The loss of interfaces

Despite the importance that our society claims to give innovation and creativity, many of the current trends in our economy limit our ability to change. The widespread imposition of quality programs, discussed further in the following chapter, by large corporate customers on their smaller suppliers reduces the ability of small companies to manage their businesses. These programs channel innovation within a much narrower range of possibilities and further centralize control of our economy.

A parallel development has been the tendency of large corporations to reduce the number of suppliers that they use in their businesses. Corporate managers often attempt to justify this movement towards fewer suppliers on the basis of increased efficiency and decreased costs. They often integrate the supplier's computer systems with those of their own company.

The supplier, sometimes with substandard wages and facilities, becomes a virtual part of the larger corporation. It is direct example of cost externalization and further reduces the freedom of the supplier to manage its business.

However, there are other, less obvious problems with the trend towards reducing the number of suppliers. These reductions carry with them costs for society as well as the companies themselves. In this case, one of these costs has been to reduce the number of relationships between employees, managers, companies, suppliers, customers, universities, governmental agencies, and so on. These relationships are the interfaces through which companies exchange information, identify needs, and create new solutions for the mutual benefit of both their companies and the greater society. Each of these interfaces is an opportunity for change and new growth.

Life often exists in its richest variety at its interfaces -- the surface of the earth, the top of the ocean, the edge of the forest, the tidal flats of the shoreline. Interfaces, such as those found in a many-stranded rope or a laminated beam, create strength. Homogeneous substances without interfaces, much like glass, often lack strength. Heterogeneous structures with multiple interfaces, such reinforcing bars in concrete or plastic laminates in windshields, possess great strength.

Port cities built on oceans or great rivers find themselves ideally located on interfaces between people enabling them to grow and prosper. Such cities have been the source of much of our economic and cultural activity. A diversity of ideas and perspectives enter these cities from distant lands that encourages innovative thinking. At the boundary, the view extends in both directions, and we can more easily appreciate both sides of an issue or question. To a certain extent, all of us live at interfaces -- in time, between the past and the future -- in space, between other people -- and in thought, between competing ideas.

In a recent column, G. Pascal Zachery noted the tendency of creative people to gravitate to the margins of life. Prophets and innovators tend to function at the interface between competing ideas. They challenge conventional thinking and offer new ways to approach old problems. For this reason, interfaces can be dangerous places for innovators as well as those affected by the innovation.

In an effort to encourage productivity and efficiency, managers often mistake interfaces for barriers. They fail to recognize the advantages of a modular structure interconnected with rich channels of communications and movement. Engineers have long acknowledged the power and flexibility of modular designs that are usually easier to design, test, and maintain.

The effect of corporate mergers is to reduce or eliminate the interfaces in our businesses and economy. There are fewer independent businesses, a smaller supplier base, and a decreased number of departments and operating units. The emphasis is on a more homogeneous management style and culture.

• The decline of economic species

In nature, wildlife depends on the appropriate habitat to survive. Research on natural ecosystems has emphasized the importance of environmental area for species diversity. A recent article suggested that a male grizzly bear needs as much as 1000 square miles of range. As development results in a loss of ecological space and habitable area decreases, there is not only a loss in the number of animals, but the variety of different species also decreases as shown in Fig. 4.

A similar problem occurs as expressways, high speed railroads, air travel, telecommunications, and the Internet contribute to the effective shrinking size of our world and the reduction of

Figure 4 - Species diversity and area

economic "area" or space available. The growth of various mega-stores and other large corporations through mergers and acquisitions as well as intense competition has reduced the economic space available for small businesses. Ultimately, we may find ourselves living in an "economic desert" in which there are few niches remaining where one can earn a living.

As a result, many economic "species" are becoming virtually extinct. Some examples include the corner grocery store, the local pharmacy, and the full service gas station. Other economic species are just hanging on. These include the mid-sized grocery store, the small bookstore, and the family farm. In today's economy, a few giant distributors dominate the retail sales of products such as toys, books, and sporting goods. Similarly, a few major suppliers dominate the production of many products from food to automobiles to computers.

The efforts of these huge distributors and suppliers to broaden their product lines to dominate even more categories compounds the problem. For example, bookstores now include a wide range of audio products as well as food served in their own cafes. Discount stores carry an immense range of products from tires to clothes and from toothpaste to garden plants. Many now include products previously carried only by much smaller specialty businesses run by professionals, such as pharmacists and optometrists, and they are increasingly adding additional product lines, such as groceries, under the same roof to form huge mega-stores. These mega-stores do not leave economic space for smaller niche marketers.

The Internet is particularly prone to this broadening of product lines. Today, customers can purchase a dazzling array of products at a number of prominent Web sites. However, the Internet, while originally touted as encouraging diversity and enabling small producers to compete more equitably, is becoming dominated by a small number of major players. Anyone can have a Web site, but only a few sites attract the majority of the shoppers. Brand recognition is proving at least as important for virtual businesses as for real stores. In addition, new Internet patents are limiting the ability of many companies to compete. The corporate world is changing the fundamental nature of the Web. The price is a decline in diversity and accessibility as the Internet evolves to serve the needs of large corporations.

From a consumer's perspective, there are now fewer independent shopping choices available. A small number of dominant suppliers own many of our most familiar brand names and determine the choices that are available in the market. It is very difficult for a smaller, independent business to obtain shelf space or Internet visibility for their products or services.

This attack on sustainable economic niches and movement toward consolidation is so strong in our society that it often threatens even powerful market leaders. Linux, a computer operating system which is available at no cost, presents a potentially serious challenge to the operating systems of the market leaders. It's difficult to lower prices sufficiently to compete with a free product. In addition, a small army of volunteers, who make the results of their labor available to anyone at no charge, continues to develop improved versions of Linux on an ad-hoc basis.

Although some people may see Linux as a positive movement away from consolidation and corporate control of software development, this perspective appears flawed for at least two reasons. First, the creators and developers of Linux receive no compensation for their efforts. For this reason, their activities more closely parallel those of the uncompensated homemaker providing a valuable service that is unrecognized as useful economic work. Second, many people who currently use Linux in their computers obtain the software through a large corporate source that packages the operating system with its own products. This enables these companies to benefit from the collective efforts of thousands of volunteers.

There are other examples of products or services that either are or could be available at little or no cost. A recent article on a failed attempt at commercializing a wireless Internet service noted that the actual cost of the service they provided was virtually nothing. The problem was covering their administrative costs. For this reason, the article suggested that we collectively consider providing free wireless access to the Internet much like rest rooms and water.

Although this is a reasonable suggestion for a devalued service, in our privatized world public rest rooms are becoming more difficult to find and purchased bottled water is replacing free drinking fountains. It seems unlikely that free wireless access to the Internet will be widely available anytime soon. Privatization often leads to an economy incapable of effectively providing goods and services that from a technological perspective could and should be available at minimal cost.

The positive aspects of the growing popularity of volunteerism, whether for Linux development or local service organizations, masks a growing devaluation of labor. The relative stagnation of factory wages is a direct manifestation of the deflationary wage environment that we have entered. In such an economy, it is very difficult for individuals to sell their services at a living wage. It becomes more difficult for individuals to survive outside of the global corporation. Economic diversity continues to decline.

This decline may be the final act in a process that began nearly two hundred years ago when home weavers found they could not compete with modern weaving machinery. A way of life that had persisted for many years abruptly ended. It is difficult to deny the ultimate benefits of the resulting gains in textile productivity. However, what were the overall human costs of these gains? How could we have managed these changes to reduce these costs?

This trend has continued with small businesses of all types being displaced by larger concerns. Today, even knowledge providers such as physicians, lawyers, stockbrokers, educators, and engineers are being affected. These professionals, who to varying degrees were self-employed in the 1800s and much of the 1900s, are now increasingly employed or controlled by large corporations.

In the process, these corporations often disempower and deskill professionals through use of the business paradigm and its associated language. The values and language of the corporate world replace the traditional values and language of their professions. Corporations refer to medical doctors as health care providers and judge them on their "productivity." Patients have become "customers." Professionals are reduced to machine-like service providers. Computer software enables them to perform their services and record their billable hours in ever smaller intervals.

The new corporate providers of these services attempt to justify these changes in the name of increased efficiency and cost savings. Although the actual dollar savings are debatable, "customers" usually find that the overall level of personal service has decreased in a variety of ways. For example, consolidations and mergers reduce the number of independent choices available to individuals while reducing the likelihood that they will continue to see the same professional and develop a long term relationship.

Part of the cause of this problem is that companies are reducing their number of employees. Such reductions generate pressures for increased productivity from each remaining employee through longer hours, busier schedules, and increased use of computers and related technology. This leads to yet more employee turnover as the remaining employees increasingly decide that they no longer want to work under these less satisfying conditions.

Corporate managements are developing new approaches to cost reductions that are affecting even highly skilled knowledge workers. In some of these knowledge fields, off-site workers can replace local employees or suppliers through the use of electronic communications and computer technology.

Some of these long distance employees are working out of their homes. While it is true that some employees find this arrangement an attractive convenience, it can lead to a variety of problems. The connections between these employees and the business are not as strong as those of the employees and managers in the office. Thus, it is easier for long distance employees to become marginalized and released at the end of a project or during a business downturn. It is more difficult for them to move up in the organization. They have less bargaining power concerning their salaries and benefits.

Other long distance workers are at the facilities of large corporations. Global corporations are using the Internet to integrate software engineers in countries with low labor costs, such as India, into their product development activities. Interactive learning and videotapes of a small number of "star" lecturers are replacing teachers. On-line trading is changing, and often reducing, the role of traditional stockbrokers. Airlines are making the life of the local travel agent more difficult. On many radio stations, either prerecorded "voice tracks" mixed with music or live "cyberjocks" or "virtual jocks" -- appearing to be local, but actually in a distant studio -- are replacing the live, local disk jockey actually playing the music.

Although these distant or on-line service providers may meet the minimal needs of the user, the many benefits of a relationship with a local, live, on-site person are missing. It becomes much more difficult to customize the services to meet local needs, to address the specific needs and questions of individuals, or to support the economic and social structure of the community.

Nearly 100 years ago, Henry Adams in his classic, *The Education of Henry Adams,* noted the tendency in capitalism toward economic concentration and domination by big money, big banks, and big corporations. He prophetically mourned the resulting loss of the educated, independent professional class of which he was a member and that we see in its final stages today. The self-employed forms of many occupations are in danger of becoming "endangered occupational species."

Despite the seeming surge in small, often home-based, business activities that often receive so much publicity, these efforts may be more of a reaction to economic consolidations and pressures than examples of economic diversity. Although some individuals intentionally decide to become consultants, many have consulting thrust upon them in varying degrees due to mergers and other downsizing activities. As such, they often serve as an additional way for corporations to externalize their costs through the outsourcing of services without having to provide long term employment and benefits. Many of these consulting businesses are quite marginal and provide limited income. They are not particularly good examples of sustainable or stable economic activity. Their owners often return to corporate employment after a relatively short stint in consulting.

Some have argued that these changes are a natural consequence of technological change and that they have happened many times before. However, we know that the collapse of species, whether biological or economic, carries with it a great deal of instability and suffering during what can be a lengthy transition. The end of the process often results in a very different world that may not have a place for many of its former occupants. Much is lost in these transformations that is worth preserving. Our evolving knowledge of DNA and genetic engineering has provided convincing evidence of the unique value of all species.

We need to recognize that diverse economic forms carry advantages that may not be immediately apparent. Small businesses including independent professionals, stores, job shops, and farmers develop specialized knowledge and practices that we lose as the standardized culture and practices of the global corporation continue to dominate our economy. These small businesses provide a flexibility that protects us in the event of unanticipated events, alternatives to a single homogeneous culture that may not meet everyone's needs, and means to evaluate concepts that are difficult to implement on a large scale.

Small businesses and other less traditional economic activities strengthen social relationships, increase the variety of job opportunities, and provide a customer base for other small businesses. They can serve as a laboratory to develop and evaluate ideas including new management practices, business concepts, technologies, and products. In the literary world, Octavio Paz in *The Other Voice* notes the creativity and diversity that small publishing houses can provide. He metaphorically compares their function to that of antibodies protecting our bodies, a good description of the role of many small businesses.

• The consequences of flawed decisions

Unfortunately, we are losing these small businesses through market actions that are deeply flawed in many ways. The market makes its decisions using limited evaluations without regard to their overall impact. Shareholders affect company valuations

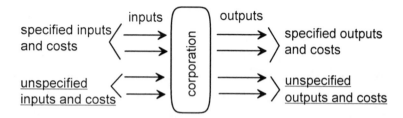

Figure 5 - Inputs and outputs of corporations

when they buy and sell stock even though they may base their decisions on little more than a sound bite, idle gossip, or simple speculation.

Quantitative analyses often use data of questionable accuracy. Financial reports are incomplete, sometimes distorted, and fail to include externalized costs that corporations have transferred to others. As shown in Fig. 5, these include the direct and indirect costs of a variety of inputs and outputs.

We ignore many inputs such as clean air and water and many outputs such as pollution simply due to tradition. In the modern world, the corporation is able to take advantage of the efforts of others to preserve and cleanup our air and water. We ignore other inputs, such as the use of our collective culture and history for such purposes as advertising and entertainment, because they are more abstract and difficult to quantify. Nonetheless, the cost of their use is to trivialize our past and damage the foundations of our future. Society pays many direct and indirect costs of corporations, costs that market decisions generally do not reflect.

On the other hand, our market decisions also ignore valuable outputs or benefits of small business or nontraditional economic activities that are difficult to convert to numbers. We consider qualitative benefits that are difficult to measure as irrelevant to our economic well being. In fact, we are often quite arbitrary in what we even consider economic activity. Our current economic system trivializes the value of activities such as housework or childcare when performed by homemakers, grandparents, or unpaid workers. For example, parents or grandparents may provide important child care services, but only the child care provided by paid providers contributes to the Gross Domestic Product.

As a consequence, parents who stay home to care for their children not only lose the financial benefits of employment, but they also forfeit their ability to cast economic "votes." We have a system that only gives economic votes to those who earn money and use it to consume goods and services. It is these votes that determine what, where, and how companies will provide various services and goods. In a society that worries about pollution, over-consumption, and energy consumption, we magnify all of these problems by only responding to the desires of those who participate in the money economy.

However, there are even more fundamental problems. In fact, the relevance of inputs and outputs to evaluating much of our economic activity is unclear. In many cases, the process itself is more important to us than the details of the economic calculations, no matter how complex. A great deal of beneficial human activity involves human interactions that are more than numbers. It is not possible to measure the inputs and outputs of these complex processes or calculate their efficiency, and yet by any reasonable definition, they contribute to our quality of life.

For example, individuals purchase products or work at jobs that seemingly make little sense using traditional economic analyses. Families make decisions concerning work both inside and outside the home based on collective preferences and desires that are difficult to quantify or explain. Volunteers use diverse and often vague explanations to explain why they enjoy volunteer work, whose actual costs and benefits, though probably impossible to quantify, are nonetheless real.

The long term health of our economy depends on maintaining a wide variety of diverse economic niches. However, as we have seen, allowing the market to make our decisions for us in a world of aggressive capitalism will not insure a diverse economy or society. The market tends to reduce everything to numbers and uses the results to determine the fate of businesses and entire communities. Applied on a global scale, the market reduces the fate of entire nations to an economic calculus that too often ignores the human needs of their people. To compound the problem, global capitalism and corporate mergers have too often replaced a diversity of players in healthy markets with tightly controlled markets dominated by a few giant corporations.

A recent panel discussion published in the *Harvard Magazine* noted that some of the economic niches and diversity that the forces of consolidation now threaten took centuries to create. Many ecologists have made similar observations about fragile environments in the natural world and have stressed the importance of protecting critical environmental niches and habitats. We must also act proactively to preserve and encourage economic and cultural diversity.

• The preservation of economic diversity

How can we encourage economic diversity? Several decades ago, Garrett Hardin in his essay, *The Tragedy of the Commons,* expressed concern over the potential misuse of shared resources that are freely available to all. He suggested that the natural tendency of each user to heavily use such a resource would inevitably lead to overuse and its destruction. The only solution seemed to be to either socialize or privatize the resource in order to control its usage.

However, there are other possibilities. Recent research by Elinor Ostrom and others has examined the sustainable use of so-called common pool resources such as shared pastureland in remote areas of Asia. Some of the pastureland in Mongolia, where self-organized local groups managed the land as shared property, was in better condition than adjacent pastureland in Russia or China controlled by either the government or by individuals. The results show that, at least in some cases, small local groups are better able to manage the use of limited common-pool resources than previously recognized. The researchers suggest that institutional diversity as well as biological diversity are important for our long term survival.

Another recent paper by Christoph Hauert and colleagues studied the social dynamics that occur during voluntary collective efforts to develop and maintain a public good (such as a common pasture). Rather than simply distinguishing between cooperators who support proper use of the pasture and defectors who exploit the pasture for their own personal advantage, they identified so-called loners who withdraw from the process, do not use the pasture, and go their own independent way.

Using a sophisticated model of this process, the authors were able to show that the participants tend to rotate their behavior between these three different roles on a dynamic basis that ultimately maintains the cooperative effort. Their research provides a possible explanation as to why cooperative groups persist despite the ability of individual members to defect and behave in ways that give them a personal advantage (as Hardin discussed in *The Tragedy of the Commons*). It again illustrates the value of a diversity of roles in our society.

As a group, dairy farmers display behavioral characteristics similar to those described by these researchers. Individual farmers may decide to sell their milk through a local farm cooperative (cooperators), they may also choose to sell their milk to a large corporation (defectors), or they may choose to abandon dairy production and pursue a niche product, such as ginseng, independent of large dairy cooperatives or corporations (loners). Consequently, the above research perhaps suggests that the long lived success of many cooperatives may be due to the continual dynamic interchange of individual farmers between their roles as cooperators, defectors, or loners.

These various research findings seem to confirm the importance of economic diversity as well as local, self-organized, cooperative groups within a community. Global corporations and national governments are unable to respond to the unique needs of each individual community. We need the flexibility inherent with economically diverse systems to address diverse, local needs. In order to ensure economic diversity within a given region, we need to empower self-organizing groups, such as cooperatives, worker collectives, land trusts, and other alternative economic structures, to guide the use of local resources and the development of the local economy.

➤ Actions to preserve economic diversity

In addition to using knowledge from economic research, we can also learn to protect and maintain economic diversity by studying the practices being used to preserve endangered wildlife species. Wildlife preserves, national parks, and other restricted areas provide protected habitats. Seed banks, zoos, and other programs enable the preservation and reintroduction of endangered species. Regulations protect species and habitats from interference by people.

We need to take comparably aggressive steps to identify endangered economic forms, to create protected economic space, and to encourage economic experimentation. We need to actively pursue policies and programs that encourage economic diversity, rather than trusting in the actions of the market. This could include actions such as the development of:

- protected economic space for small businesses through the use of zoning and other ordinances;

- improved regulations that recognize the impact of company size;

- progressive taxation policies based on the ability to pay;

- new accounting practices that reflect the impact of the overall inputs/costs and outputs/benefits of a business;

- governmental oversight of standards to encourage innovation and accommodate small businesses;

- improved access to health and disability insurance for small businesses and nontraditional workers;

- increased participation for those outside of the traditional economy in our decision-making processes;

- alternative economic forms such as neighborhood groups, community farms, and cooperatives;

- educational programs that recognize the value of a variety of management styles;

- fewer subsidies for large corporations and more financial incentives to encourage small businesses;

- restrictions on the ability of companies to control other suppliers through language in purchasing contracts;

- increased understanding of the impact of corporate mergers and absentee owners on our communities; and

- economic impact reviews to mitigate the impact of mergers and other major economic decisions on the local community.

The following chapters will present detailed discussions of many of these proposals as well as additional suggestions to enable us to regain control of our economy and society.

CHAPTER 4

Return to Adaptive Management

In recent years, many managers and corporations have embraced quality management programs that reflect their belief that strong controls are the route to accomplishing their goals. The recent behavior of some property owners in northern Wisconsin illustrated the futility of attempting to impose rigid controls over our world. In an effort to preserve their view of the water, they aggressively cut back the underbrush. Rather than selectively pruning to encourage the growth of specific trees and control the growth of undesired shrubs and weeds, they simply sheared everything to a uniform height. In the short run, this approach quickly and easily creates a neat and tidy appearance. However, in the long run, it results in an impenetrable thicket of branches. It symbolizes the rigid, and often ineffective, bureaucracy that emerges in an organization that overemphasizes controls and standardization.

* * *

Management by Control

Throughout the first half of the twentieth century, management evolved in a way that paralleled the technological successes of the era. The development of so-called "scientific management," most usually associated with the work of Frederick Winslow Taylor, was often successful in increasing efficiencies and improving production for processes that featured well-defined, slowly changing work flows. However, these efforts carried a human cost that Taylor debated in congressional hearings in his day and that others have continued to debate to the present time. The focus of many of these arguments was his own claim that the system came ahead of the individual.

Today, many quality management perspectives reflect the spirit of Taylor's early work. They carry a wide variety of labels including Total Quality Management (TQM), the Deming method, the Baldrige Criteria, Six Sigma, and many others. Despite these different names and many differences in detail, these programs have many similarities. Most significantly, they often include the use of advanced statistical techniques, continuous improvement processes, and customer driven activities. Although these various techniques have received deserved recognition as useful methods to improve productivity and product quality, they raise many concerns.

Reflecting their technical heritage, most of these programs are weak in terms of their people focus. They take a mechanistic approach that is quantitative in form as well as content. Most of these quality programs overemphasize the importance of measurement, again reflecting their engineering heritage. In fact, the National Institute of Standards and Technology (NIST) administers the Baldrige Award program. Thus, the same agency that determines our units of physical measurement recognizes companies for their management practices.

There is also an ideological dimension to scientific management practices that critics have questioned since the days of Taylor. The stated goals of these program include increased profits for the shareholders and improved products for the customers. The benefits for the workers are less certain. Today, it is not even clear that customer driven programs are in the customer's best interests. It is often difficult for customers to make informed requests or evaluations of products because of their lack of familiarity with the manufacturing, engineering, and technology of the product they are using.

However, beyond these specific issues, there is a more fundamental problem. Management systems since Taylor have too often reflected a reductionist approach to business management. This approach considers the whole to be the sum of its parts and uses the concepts of linear systems theory to break the job or business into its component elements. It then optimizes the performance of the system using the measurement of the inputs and outputs of each element. As mentioned previously, it is not easy to define or measure the inputs and outputs of many jobs and processes. This is especially true for knowledge workers, and, as noted by Peter Drucker, it is not at all clear how to improve their overall effectiveness.

Linear systems theory evolved from engineering studies of machines and systems. For linear systems, when we double the input, we find that the output is also twice as large. Engineers often make the assumption of linearity, since it is reasonable for many specific technical problems and greatly simplifies the mathematical analysis. Nonetheless, it often resembles looking under the streetlight for a lost object because that is where the light is brightest. Similarly, most management approaches depict the organization as a black box in which the outputs have a fixed, linear relationship to the inputs as shown in Fig. 6.

The actual world in which we work and live is not a linear system; it displays nonlinear behavior. The whole is rarely equal to the sum of its parts. For example, the output might be proportional to the square of the input. In such a nonlinear system, when we double the input, we find that the output is four times as large.

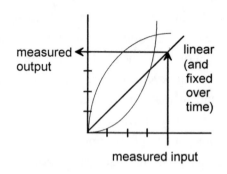

    The nonlinear nature of many systems often results in complex behavior that appears to be random and chaotic. However, quasiperiodic, though unpredictable, patterns can appear in these systems which are a result of their nonlinear characteristics. Physicists

Figure 6 - Typical assumptions for linear systems analysis. The real world is nonlinear, see curved lines above, and changes with time.

sometimes describe these complex patterns as "emergent" properties of the system. They occur for systems that are more lively or dynamic than a relatively stationary system (such as a gentle stream), and less chaotic than a totally turbulent system (such as a fast moving rapids). The classic example is a dribbling faucet that does not have the regularity of a steady drip nor the complete chaos of a rushing stream. Similarly, many of the most interesting aspects of life, including life itself, occur in the intermediate condition between complete stability and complete chaos.

    In addition to the nonlinear relationship of many inputs and outputs in the real world, the specific form of these relationships also changes over time. Systems analysis commonly assumes that the relationship between the input and output of a system does not change. Furthermore, economic analyses usually reflect the value of specific measurements at discrete points of time. However, the analysis of a discrete series of points cannot adequately describe the important characteristics and results of most human activities. Events occur rapidly, unpredictably, and continuously with time. As a result, rigid rules and procedures quickly become obsolete. Last week's rules and procedures are often inadequate to deal with this week's problems and questions. Businesses need a more realistic and flexible approach to management.

Adaptive Approaches to Management

• Small businesses and adaptive management

There are alternatives to the frantic pace and rigid controls of the modern corporate world. Many small businesses are very effective in carrying out their mission despite their often more relaxed pace and lack of extensive rules and procedures. Instead of complex managerial systems, they build on the inherent strengths of employees able to perform the required tasks of the business. They demonstrate an intuitive understanding of how to manage a business. They use a more flexible, adaptive style of management.

Nelson displayed the power of decentralized, flexible management principles on a regular basis. The company empowered its employees and managers to act decisively in moving the company's programs ahead with a minimum of bureaucracy. Similarly, the early organization of Digisonix was quite fluid, and personnel often moved between the corporate research group and Digisonix as necessary to meet the daily needs of the two organizations. This type of fluid structure is one of the key advantages of the culture and approach of many small businesses. It differs in significant ways from management techniques emphasizing the use of controls and standards that are the descendants of scientific management.

• Background on adaptive systems

This decentralized, flexible management style of small businesses reflects many of the characteristics of what have come to be known as adaptive systems. Adaptive systems use a simple collection of guidelines that enables them to function effectively even in a rapidly changing and unpredictable world.

The theory of adaptive systems traces its development from attempts to model the behavior of the neurons in our brains. Neurons communicate with their neighbors and modify their collective behavior in response to past experiences. Thus, adaptive systems theory has its origins in biology and nature rather than the world of electrical and mechanical machines. In fact, the field now known as "neural networks" evolved from early research on adaptive systems. Perhaps it is not surprising that adaptive systems theory provides a more powerful metaphor for effective management than linear systems theory.

An adaptive process continually modifies its behavior using a small number of simple rules to achieve the desired behavior in the face of a changing world. Each adjustment, although quite small in itself, incorporates the effects of many events, interactions, connections, and changes that are typical of the world in which we live.

Adaptive, or self-organizing, systems have the ability to respond very rapidly to changing conditions. They often operate on the verge of complete instability or the edge of chaos. These systems modify their performance in response to their surroundings to meet a desired goal. They do this through the use of continuous feedback and memory that seeks to capture the results of past experience and incorporate them into future behavior. The adaptive process features:

- many semi-independent elements,
- decentralized control of each element,
- use of multiple inputs,
- continuous feedback of performance,
- small number of rules,
- many small adjustments to behavior,
- remembering all experiences,
- rich interconnections with other elements,
- continuous self-learning.

The resulting behavior is often complex and seemingly random. However, patterns gradually emerge that reflect the desired behavior.

Considering the biological motivations behind adaptive systems theory, it is not surprising that people as well as the organizations that they create often function most effectively using principles that closely resemble those studied in adaptive systems research. Effective organizations use a small number of clear guidelines or rules applied with continuous real time feedback to create a self-correcting, self-learning, adaptive organization as illustrated in Fig. 7.

Adaptive management encourages this process and differs from more traditional management styles in its emphasis on learning by doing. An adaptive management style allows employees to use their own initiative in many small ways to help the organization achieve its goals.

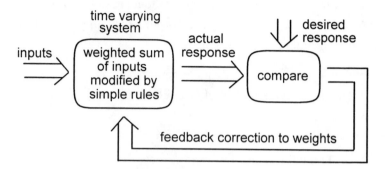

Figure 7 - Basic elements of adaptive systems
(corrections are small and occur rapidly)

As mentioned earlier, the managers of small businesses often display an intuitive grasp of these principles and empower their employees to effectively perform a wide variety of jobs whenever the need arises. Managers of larger corporations often find themselves trapped within a system and culture that attempts to control behavior in a huge organization with its many products and locations through the use of rigid procedures and controls.

• The adaptive organization

The emphasis in the adaptive organization is on using the unique knowledge, skills, and experiences of each employee. People are part of the living world and bring with them the strength, robustness, and vitality of natural processes. Adaptive management approaches treat employees as people, rather than machines. The unique strengths, contributions, and needs of each individual combine to create a more robust, action-oriented organization. Engineers often speak of the different "degrees of freedom" required to model and control a complex system. In the same manner, the diverse capabilities of many employees combine to produce the desired results for the organization in a rapidly changing world.

At Nelson, employees were routinely gaining new skills in engineering, manufacturing, project management, accounting, marketing, personnel management, corporate finance, and many other areas. Nelson tried to increase employees skills to make them more versatile, but not necessarily interchangeable. It also tried to utilize its employees as fully as possible, regardless of their education. In fact, there were many examples of highly effective contributors at Nelson who had a relatively limited amount of formal education.

In most global corporations, it is common to find many employees with a great deal of formal education. However, the trend, often driven by so-called quality programs, towards standardized jobs and procedures can result in the under utilization of this education. In fact, employees can actually become deskilled by programs that restrict the application of their current knowledge.

Nelson also made good use of the skills of its managers. The company encouraged and expected them to make decisions. In addition, Nelson had a flat organization in which managers were doers. This approach kept them out of the way of other employees, allowed them to create value through their personal efforts, and helped make them better managers. Since the managers were busy with their own personal projects and professional contributions, they encouraged their employees to use their own professional skills. There was less time and energy for bureaucracy. There was more time for learning and doing.

Global corporations often enmesh managers in a large, complex structure in which there are so many meetings, requests, and deadlines that there is little time for personal contributions or initiatives. Instead, managers spend their time serving the system. In fact, to meet numerous external demands and deadlines, managers may need to request support from their employees that actually interferes with the employees' personal assignments. It again brings to mind, Galbraith's comment on the tendency of corporate managers to delegate thinking and problem-solving to others. There often is simply no time for any other alternative.

Unfortunately, corporate managers often do not recognize or adequately value the skills and experience of their employees. When they encounter a noteworthy achievement, particularly if it is outside of the normal corporate structure in a "boot leg" or "skunk works" project, managers often simply attribute the success to luck. They insist that corporate style procedures and bureaucracy are essential to successful programs. They fail to adequately recognize the time, talent, and effort required to learn and practice a craft or profession. The impact of luck is only in the context of extensive preparations and considerable hard work. In a contest between flexible talent and rigid bureaucracy, flexible talent will win almost every time.

This preference of many corporate managers for systems over talent has implications for the hiring and retention of employees. If success is mainly due to skills and experience, corporations will highly value capable employees and work very hard to retain them. However, if success is mainly due to luck, corporations can easily replace employees by anyone who would be just as likely to be "lucky" in the future. This may be the reason that some managers overemphasize luck and outside elements as the primary factors in an individual's contributions rather than experience, skill, and effort. Such a view makes the employee expendable and the system essential.

This tendency to diminish the importance of the individual can contribute to the inability of some individuals to recognize their own inherent value. They lock themselves into jobs, marriages, friendships, or other relationships that have turned destructive to them and those around them. They see the relationship as the source of their identity rather than recognizing their own unique value as an individual. They may feel that they need to maintain the relationship to avoid devaluing the past and losing their own identity. For this reason, it takes great courage to leave a relationship that is unhealthy, controlling, disempowering, or invalidating -- and to start over.

In the economic arena, the lack of self-respect also makes it more difficult for individuals to deal with the problems that they may face in their work. Industrial workers who lose their jobs through business slowdowns or corporate mergers often blame themselves for their misfortune. Similarly, farmers who either sell their farms or declare bankruptcy, often feel like they have failed even though it is often deep flaws within the system that are most responsible for their difficulties.

- **The role of memory**

One of the most important ingredients in an adaptive learning process is the use of a rich memory combined with continuous feedback. The collective experience and history of an organization are important because they contain valuable information that helps to predict, control, and affect the future. In general, complex desired behavior requires the continual addition and retention of information. This infusion of knowledge parallels the way in which most of us try to learn from our mistakes. The collective experiences of the employees, along with various files and databases of the organization, provide the primary depositories for long term corporate memory.

In addition, the use of performance feedback to influence future actions provides additional short term memory for the organization. Individuals collect information on current performance and transfer this information to other members of the organization who modify the system to improve overall performance. This ability to quickly process new information through the use of long and short term memory in order to optimize performance is a unique advantage of adaptive systems. A rigid process cannot adjust to change and allows organizations to get left behind by rapidly changing circumstances.

Given that many of the popular quality initiatives are supposedly data driven, it is ironic that many businesses seem to often devalue the experiences of their older employees. The experiences embedded in the individual memories of these workers represent valuable data for the business that is at least as important as the specific measurements resulting from statistical quality control programs. Despite efforts to attempt to codify this knowledge and experience, it is impossible to capture all of the expertise of an experienced individual in the pages of a book. This is why students study under a master to learn many crafts and trades and why universities still emphasize the role of the advisor for a student, particularly in graduate study.

In his recent novel, *Slowness,* Milan Kundera notes the connection between speed and memory. He suggests that people slow down when they are trying to remember and speed up when they are trying to forget. The behavior of the global corporation is often quite similar. Operating at high speed, it has little use for a past that it seems to be trying to forget. We now understand that adaptive systems are quite different. Much like people, their effectiveness comes from their ability to incorporate all past experiences as they move incrementally towards the desired result.

Some successful organizations are now realizing that the skills and experiences of employees are important. The past does matter. We learn from the past. We build on the past. Human beings are the integrated sum of their experiences. Rather than considering the past irrelevant, we should recognize it as the source of our unique strengths. Adaptive systems attain their impressive performance by utilizing all previous information. Similarly, we need to recognize the power of using the past to build the future.

• **The empowered employee**

This desired behavior naturally emerges in an adaptively managed organization through the combined result of the efforts of many diverse individuals. Ironically, the organization achieves its goals by "letting go" of total control and encouraging all of its members to take charge. Of course, there is still a need for a certain amount of structure including standards, procedures, and rules, but structure alone will not produce the desired results. Success is more likely when we combine structure with employees that we empower to deal with the wide variety of problems encountered in any business.

These characteristics of good management practices have much in common with good parenting skills. Children do not become complete, strong adults if parents raise them with a lengthy rule book. There are never enough rules to cover all present, much less future situations. It is better to focus on a few basic guidelines and create an open, communications intensive style that allows children to adapt to a given situation. Desired behavior results as a natural consequence of empowering children to make their own decisions. Children are naturally very good at this process. Watch any baby learning to walk -- new attempts quickly follow every fall and before long, the baby is running through the house -- all accomplished with little, if any direct instruction.

We can observe similar behavior in many team sports where success often depends upon a good game plan as well as individual initiative and adaptability. For example, a football team usually has a series of predetermined plays, but the individual players also need to adaptively respond to the actions of the opposing team. This may involve the quarterback scrambling to get free or a receiver deviating from the specified pattern to get open. In both cases, the player follows the simple rule to seek an open area. The ability to function adaptively when faced with an unanticipated situation is what often marks a superior team. A set of plays and rules for the players is necessary, but not sufficient for maximum effectiveness.

Despite the current trend to use rigid controls and procedures in the corporate world, organizations in other fields often make effective use of more adaptive approaches to management. For example, a recent paper by Robert Pool described the organizational structures used on a large aircraft carrier. It seems that under routine operation, the crew follows a traditional hierarchical management structure. However, during critical procedures, such as the launching and recovery of aircraft, they adopt a much more cooperative and interactive approach that appears to share many of the characteristics of an adaptive management style.

Unfortunately, many managers, particularly in larger organizations, do not appreciate the advantages of empowered employees managed using adaptive principles. They prefer to control and standardize all aspects of the business including the behavior of their employees. They believe this will enable them to achieve their goals. Although this may be possible for some businesses in the short term, it is not effective in a long run. Excessive control creates an organization that loses the strength that comes with flexibility.

Sadly, there are also some employees who prefer a control oriented style of management. It allows the individual to avoid personal responsibility for their actions or inactions. They simply have to follow the rules and let the system take the blame. However, there are consequences for both the individual and the organization from taking this approach. Both the organization and the individual will fall short of achieving their full potential. Ultimately, this attitude can lead to personal bitterness, financial losses, legal problems, and even business failures.

A recent column by David Greising discussed the large training facility operated by Arthur Andersen, the giant accounting firm involved with the collapse of Enron. He reported that one of the primary goals of the training center was to create standardized, interchangeable employees able to work effectively throughout the Andersen organization. He further noted that one of the downsides to this approach is that it may lead to an excessive emphasis on conformity and to an unwillingness to ask the hard questions within an organization. A greater emphasis on the need to question and challenge the organization might have helped avoid some of the problems that resulted from Andersen's work with Enron.

In contrast to conformity, adaptive management stresses the need for each employee to question and react to each situation that they encounter. The emphasis is on individual initiative with continual evaluation of performance and modification of behavior to meet the company's stated goals.

The Future of Adaptive Management

Interestingly, there are also some indications that the seemingly unbounded enthusiasm for quality management programs may be moderating. A recent commentary in a leading engineering magazine noted that a survey of senior executives reported a decline in the use of Total Quality Management (TQM) tools. Although post-survey interviews attributed the decline to the number of opportunities available in the current strong economy, it may also reflect a growing recognition of the limitations of these quality management programs.

For instance, a number of writers have noted the difficulties involved in the use of TQM practices in a rapidly changing, unpredictable work environment. Of course, most businesses today find these to be the very environments that are most common. Adaptive approaches offer significant advantages in these areas. Even in product engineering environments where quality management programs can be essential in documenting mature production processes properly, their utility is open to question when the processes are not yet mature.

Recently, a variety of books and articles have begun to appear that recognize the power of adaptive principles for management. As reflected in many of these books and articles, adaptive approaches to management that utilize the strengths of decentralized control and self-organizing behavior are a powerful way to improve the speed of response and productivity in large companies or projects. However, beyond speed and productivity, adaptive management techniques offer other advantages in improving the effectiveness of an organization.

Adaptive management creates a culture that uses the natural strengths of employees to build stronger businesses. Managers encourage employees to work towards the basic goals of the company rather than serve the demands of the corporate system. Corporate systems are fine and needed, but as many small businesses have long recognized, they should serve the company and its employees, rather than the other way around. The result is an organization that is more responsive to customer needs and better able to respond to unexpected events.

Perhaps the most important step we can take in managing our companies and redirecting the goals of our society is to recognize the futility and ineffectiveness of our obsessive pursuit of control. The desire of managers and investors to gain greater control of the future of their business and industry drives many corporate mergers. They operate under the illusion that they can improve their ability to control their future by increasing the size of their businesses.

After these mergers, they seek to impose their control by instituting centralized managerial authority and standardized systems and policies. As we have seen in this chapter, such efforts at absolute control are ultimately ineffective. As shown by the recent collapse of a number of giant corporations, the centralized corporate management model is no guarantee for success. In fact, small companies and organizations using a more flexible, decentralized management approach have often proven to be more vital and sustainable than larger corporations.

Unfortunately, the same desire for control drives the legalistic nature of our society and its skyrocketing incarceration rates. We pass legislation that increases our prison populations at a time when overall crime rates have generally declined. Seeking simple solutions for complex problems, initial demands for "three strikes and you're out" judicial standards have now become calls for "one strike and you're out." In light of recent revelations of instances of child abuse within the church, even some church leaders are now supporting such a policy.

These trends fail to recognize that throughout our lives, we are continually facing a broad diversity of problems that deserve individual and thoughtful responses. Nonetheless, many people hope that standardized, legalistic, and punitive responses will somehow help them to gain control over a society that they see as "out of control."

Ironically, at the same time that many seek to apply greater controls on employees and the general public, our leaders continue to deregulate our economy, remove constraints on corporations, and pursue so-called free trade policies.

Throughout this period, the democratic process has suffered. We have allowed the political process to become dominated by large contributors and have agreed to international trade proceedings that often operate behind closed doors. As a result, we have a relatively small number of individuals gaining ever increasing control over our economy and society while seeking to further concentrate their personal power and wealth.

We need to find a better balance between our use of societal rules and individual judgment. Recent events have demonstrated that in some economic and political areas, we need more structure and regulations. However, in many other areas of social behavior, we need to rely less on rigid responses to what are often complex problems and more on thoughtful evaluations of each case on an individual basis.

Fundamentally, this will require a change in our values. In the language of the Christian church, we need to move beyond Old Testament values based on law to New Testament values based on grace. In secular terms, we need to move from controlling to caring.

➤ Guidelines for adaptive management

Although small businesses perhaps lend themselves more readily to an adaptive approach to management, there is no reason why larger corporations and organizations cannot also adopt many of its principles. This will, however, require the managers of these larger companies to:

- find a new balance between control and trust;

- focus on action rather than analysis;

- understand the value of decentralized management;

- listen to their experienced employees and build on their knowledge; and

- empower employees to make the many, small decisions that characterize the adaptive organization.

These characteristics are closely related to the desire of many large companies to become more nimble and quick as they struggle with the competitive demands of the current global economy. As discussed above, these techniques also have their roots in the culture of small businesses. Unfortunately, we are losing many of these small businesses through continuing corporate mergers and the dominance of large corporations. It is another reason why it is important to preserve small businesses and economic diversity of all kinds.

CHAPTER 5

The Quest for Justice

Towering trees surround the spectacular Capitol of Wisconsin high on an isthmus between Lakes Mendota and Monona. The exterior is a classical design of brilliant white stone. The interior is alive with wonderful paintings and exquisite carvings of stone of many different colors. The beauty of the building reflects the values of an earlier era when public buildings were a priority.

To the east are much newer government buildings that stress functionality more than aesthetics. Tiny cubicles jam their plain interiors. There is little evidence of the pride in government displayed in the Capitol building.

A few blocks to the west of the capitol is the main campus of the University of Wisconsin. An eclectic collection of buildings -- some new, many old, and all quite crowded -- press together for more than a mile along the shore of Lake Mendota. Although still impressive, the cramped, often older buildings suggest that education is no longer a top priority.

Several miles farther west is the home of the University Research Park. This extensive development features gentle hills, curving drives, large sites, beautiful landscaping, and many attractive new buildings housing a variety of businesses, some of which grew out of university research. It clearly demonstrates the central role that business has taken in our society. Our architecture reflects our values.

* * *

Concern for the Future

O ver the past 20 years, our society seems to have lost much of its passion for justice and its concern for the future. Two decades ago, there was an intense amount of interest in such issues as population growth, resource shortages, and economic justice. In the late 1970s, international conferences, such as *Alternatives to Growth '77* and *The Management of Sustainable Growth*, continued the discussion begun with the publication of the report, *The Limits to Growth*, in 1972. The attendees included a broad range of governmental, educational, and business leaders. At about the same time, President Jimmy Carter directed preparation of the *Global 2000* report on similar topics.

In the early 1980s, regional conferences in Wisconsin, such the *Consultation on Ethics and Energy* in Stevens Point as well as *Power, Poverty, and Politics* in Madison, explored local concerns and problems in a time of declining resources and economic turmoil. A few years later, the seminar, *Act on the Word* in Green Lake focused on social ministry and public policy, while *Economic Problems and Policy* in Madison emphasized economic justice issues.

Unfortunately, as the 1980s continued to unfold followed by the booming 1990s, interest in these issues seemed to gradually give way to emerging interest in the stock market, the Internet, and books on how to become a millionaire. Today, many people are too young to remember the concern for important environmental and economic issues that existed in the late 1970s and early 1980s. Others virtually ridicule the visionary concerns for the future that President Carter expressed at that time. There still is little sense of urgency about the continuing rapid growth of population in many parts of the world, growing problems with energy resources, widespread water shortages, threatening environmental problems, and the growing gap between the rich and poor.

Despite the need for global attention on these problems, the Bush administration has adopted an independent posture that is often at odds with the views of many other countries. Among the most prominent examples have been its positions on global warming, missile defense treaties, and globalization of the world's economy. In particular, according to a recent article by R. C. Longworth, many non-American delegates to the recent World Economic Forum doubt whether the current administration understands the connection between current protests regarding globalization and the serious economic inequities that exist throughout the world. Forum delegates, except for a few Americans, reportedly believe that the future of the global economy depends upon taking steps to insure that the poor share in the world's prosperity.

Longworth's article also notes an unusual shift that has occurred in the international debate on globalization. Prior to the attacks on the World Trade Center, protesters staged confrontations at most international meetings on economics to object to the effects of globalization and the impact of various free trade treaties. Many governmental leaders reacted with disdain. Barbed wire and riot police met protesters' attempts to open up the discussion of these issues. As a consequence of the violence that sometimes occurred, the press gave protesters and their message substantial coverage. Although the publicity was welcome, over time, activists came to recognize this as a mixed blessing since their message sometimes got lost in the ugly aftermath of some of the violence.

Following the September 11 attacks, protesters, at least in this country, have toned down the level of their protests resulting in less press coverage. Nonetheless, even economic insiders are now beginning to voice concerns about the need to address economic inequities that undermine global peace and unity. Surprisingly, and perhaps encouragingly, a number of speakers at the recent World Economic Forum echoed some of the complaints of the protesters at the same time that the press is giving them less publicity. Yet, considerable doubt remains as to whether this recognition of some problems by a few leaders will actually lead to substantive reform of the overall globalization process.

The Religion of the Market

Indeed, much of our society continues to express an obsessive faith in using market costs and prices to direct our decisions. Market directed decisions justify shortsighted energy and environmental policies, extraordinary salaries for a select few, and the production of the cheapest possible products. Market directed decisions even direct our personal decisions on careers, purchases, and investments. The market relieves us of the need to take responsibility for our lives and make our own decisions for the direction of our society.

The theologian, Harvey Cox, recently wrote in *The Atlantic Monthly* about our tendency to view the "market" as having characteristics usually only ascribed to God. These include being omnipotent, omniscient, and omnipresent. We trust the market even though, as noted by Octavio Paz in *The Other*

Voice, it is unable to set a direction or to make choices based on any values or criteria other than prices. Perhaps our willingness to ascribe Godlike power and knowledge to the market unwittingly reflects our own difficulties in creating a clear vision for our world.

In our market driven mentality, all aspects of life become economic commodities with an economic value assigned by the market. The numbers drive the economy, and the economy drives our society. We focus on who or what is bigger, faster, or richer. If we can't convert it into a number in a spreadsheet, we ignore it. Using computers to weight and sum our numbers, we avoid having to make our own decisions. In a rather extreme example, an engineering friend of mine used this technique to determine the location of his retirement home. Most people would probably find living in a community for a few months more useful than any spreadsheet evaluation.

A recent article even described efforts to quantify the evaluation of student writing using a six trait scheme and a five point scale. In this computational world, there is little room for dreams, creativity, art, love, or the many other qualities that are important aspects of our humanity. There is plenty of room, however, for the development of criteria in the rating process to control the student's expression of ideas.

Our obsession with numbers sometimes turns up in the most surprising areas. A recent article described efforts at a church to improve participation of their members in a Bible study program. Every week, the church leaders used a different number to encourage involvement. One week the number was 350 reflecting the goal to get 350 members involved, another week the number was 45 reflecting the goal to meet 45 minutes each week, the next week the number was 40 reflecting the desire for 40 leaders for the study groups, and so on. While the simplicity of numbers may be a way to catch people's attention in a busy world, people also respond to words, and the church is one place where words seem more appropriate than numbers.

Nowhere is our obsession with numbers more evident than in our apparent need to separate the world into winners and losers. We live in what Robert Frank and Philip Cook described in their book as a "winner takes all" society. We seem to have an obsessive focus on "gold" medals. People too often devalue the abilities of the second place finisher. The various state-run lotteries use games based on a multitude of numbers to generate one big winner who receives a huge financial prize. Television game shows feature various competitions with ordinary people trying to strike it rich. Televised sports activities focus viewer's attention on a mountain of numerical data to determine the champions and winners of various competitions. On the political scene, the 2000 presidential election evolved into an intense numerical battle eventually resolved by a 5 to 4 decision to determine the winner.

Competition can be enjoyable and useful, but cooperation is also important. Many of our most important institutions including families, schools, churches, and hospitals are the results of cooperative efforts. Even our highly competitive businesses owe their existence to the cooperative actions of the managers and employees. Throughout nature, in addition to competition for food, territory, and mates, we find dependence on symbiotic relationships in which multiple organisms win together. Cooperation may be less exciting than the intensity of competition, but it plays a critical, often under appreciated role in life.

In contrast, we are paying a significant cost due to our obsession with competition and winning. We are sending the discouraging message that there is no reason to compete except to win a gold medal. If you can't be the best, why try anything? We are also losing our ability to compromise or to strive for consensus. Why compromise, if winning is everything?

At a deeper level, our emphasis on winners helps justify the wealth accumulated by the most affluent members of our society. The lotteries, game shows, and books on millionaires all suggest that through a combination of hard work or good fortune anyone can become wealthy. For this reason, they imply that it is perfectly acceptable for there to be a few big winners, a somewhat larger number of near winners, and a much larger number of so-called losers relegated to the back seat.

In the name of political and social expediency, these simplistic messages ignore the host of societal policies and historical realities that limit the potential of many members of our society. Our society provides inherent advantages for those in control. Political power accompanies economic wealth. This power has created a system that uses language, literacy requirements, economic barriers, voting restrictions, complex regulations, trade practices, and other means to prevent people from fully participating in our economic, political, and social systems. Racial discrimination, class prejudice, and religious intolerance further hinder the efforts of millions to succeed. Yet, we still find many of the winners in our society using the presumed objectivity of the market and a winner takes all attitude to justify their success and to ignore the various inequities in our society.

In addition to these moral considerations, our obsession with winning also has other consequences. In the world of business, it leads to little concern for the culture of an acquired firm following a merger. After all, they lost, didn't they? In addition to the human cost of this attitude, it can threaten the ultimate success of the business merger itself. The culture of an acquired business was an integral part of the success that was presumably one of the primary reasons that the acquiring firm decided to merge with it. In order to sustain this success, the new corporate owners should recognize the key role played by business culture and introduce any changes to this culture gradually and with careful deliberation. This will help retain employees and increase the likelihood of a successful merger.

Despite the obsession of the market with numbers and winners, we continue to trust it to guide the actions of our economy. The recent power crisis in California following deregulation of the electrical power industry provides a good example. It should cast some doubt in the hearts and minds of even the most enthusiastic supporters of the market. Some proponents of deregulation claim that the problems were primarily due to environmental regulations and resistance to new power plants. Although these factors may have contributed to the problem, there were also other important factors. It appears that the players in the market were also reluctant to propose or build new power plants, due to perceived uncertainties in a deregulated market. As a result, the market failed to provide adequate power. Meanwhile, the new owners of the now deregulated power plants enjoyed huge increases in their profits.

There is also widespread speculation that some owners of existing power plants may have manipulated the supply of power to increase prices. The withdrawal of the power from selected power plants can have a much larger impact than might be expected. Due to limitations of the power distribution grid, certain regions are heavily dependent upon nearby power plants. When the power from these plants is unavailable, it can be impossible to make up the difference with power from other regions. In fact, one source reported that rolling blackouts occurred in California when the state had 55,000 kilowatts of capacity with an overall demand of only 31,000 kilowatts.

Problems with deregulation of the electrical power industry demonstrate the weakness of the market system in meeting needs that require long term planning or the cooperation of many diverse players, but there are many others. A recent article touted the contributions of the private sector to the success of the early communications satellite known as *Telstar* while minimizing the role of the government in creating the launch vehicles and related infrastructure. It is unlikely that the private sector acting alone in response to market needs could have created these capabilities. Similar comments apply to many other innovations that now have broad commercial value. One of the most noteworthy is the Internet which evolved from the government-sponsored Arpanet, developed in the late 1960s with funding from the Department of Defense's Advanced Research Projects Agency (ARPA).

The failure of the market system to respond to our critical societal need for vaccines provides a more recent example. Problems have ranged from late deliveries of flu vaccines, delays in the production of vaccines related to bioterrorism, and shortages of important vaccines for childhood diseases. Normal market forces based on supply and demand have been inadequate to prevent many suppliers from leaving the field due to technological challenges, small market size, inadequate profitability, and legal liability.

Although the market system has many advantages and has effectively met many of our societal needs, its problems and shortcomings should cause all of us to question our willingness to allow it to make virtually all of our societal decisions. As we have seen, even under ideal circumstances it fails to consider many factors that are critical to building a successful, sustainable society. Under real world conditions, the market is subject to distortions due to the unequal distribution of power and wealth between people as well as outright manipulation, cheating, and deception by some individuals.

Even insiders in the financial world are beginning to concede the need for strong actions to solve problems that the market cannot address by itself. Following the collapse of Enron, many people began to question the adequacy of our financial reporting system. A recent report from Merrill Lynch in discussing these concerns noted that, in addition to market forces, regulatory and legal forces have often played a role in achieving needed reforms in the past. Current reform efforts in Congress, regulatory agencies, and the financial industry will likely further strengthen these controls. Nonetheless, our collective faith in the market remains strong. We invariably blame extraneous factors for economic debacles rather than admit that despite the obvious strengths of the market system, it is an imperfect system.

The Growth of Economic Injustice

Unfortunately, we use our seemingly unbounded faith in market economics and financial analyses too often to strengthen the rich and powerful rather than improve the lives of the poor and weak. In some cases, such as the California power crisis, the process is quite obvious. A relatively small number of companies that owned the power plants enjoyed huge increases in their profits, while the huge base of rate payers will likely see increased rates despite no added value for the consumer.

In other cases, the process is less obvious, but the results are more far reaching. For example, one of the persistent problems in market economies has been the emergence of price inflation sometimes caused by an imbalance in supply and demand. Although extreme inflation can discourage savings and hurt those on fixed incomes, a moderate level of inflation does not appear to cause significant problems. However, inflation does generally favor working debtors at the expense of wealthy creditors. Perhaps for this reason, the wealthy and powerful often pressure the government to control inflation through economic measures that harm the average worker.

Despite these concerns with inflation in the prices of goods and services, there are other forms of inflation that do not trigger the same reactions from those in control of the economic levers. No one seemed particularly disturbed by the inflationary increases in the market prices of shares of stock in the 1990s. The business world called the resulting extraordinary increases in personal wealth simply the rewards of a good investment. Inflationary increases in income are apparently less offensive when they result from your investments rather than your personal labor -- the result is a double standard on inflation.

Nonetheless, articles suggested that the rise in stock prices did indeed fuel a steady increase in overall consumer spending during this period. The increases in spending varied between individuals, since the rising stock market affected individuals in different ways. The average person benefited from rising stock prices at most through increases in their retirement accounts. Their accessible financial wealth didn't change significantly. However, wealthy individual investors saw a dramatic rise in their personal wealth. These gains undoubtedly contributed to the strong demand and rapid price increases in the 1990s for luxury homes, second homes, and other high end products. The net effect was still more concentration of individual wealth.

Much like our distorted view of investment returns, business articles usually do not describe the dramatic increases in the income of the CEOs of many companies as inflationary. On the other hand, many of our business leaders and analysts express alarm at the prospect of raising the wages of our lowest income citizens. They often resist efforts to raise the minimum wage, which has fallen far behind the cost of living. In fact, even factory wages in Wisconsin have failed to keep pace with inflation over the past twenty years. This parallels the trend for overall wages shown in Fig. 8.

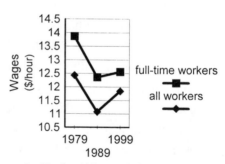

Figure 8 - Median Wisconsin hourly wages (1999$; see COWS using CPS data, 2000a)

When decreasing unemployment causes wages and inflation to begin to increase, the Federal Reserve Bank often quickly moves to increase interest rates. It hopes that this will reduce demand for labor, keep wages down, and reduce inflation. At about this same time, in a tone often solemn and pedagogical, the media usually instructs us that of course companies can only increase wages if the productivity of the workers increases by a similar amount.

Productivity is a red herring that analysts often bring forth to forestall requests for wage increases or other benefits for the least powerful members of our society. We virtually never hear any reports about the relationship between earnings and productivity for senior managers. Instead, the emphasis is invariably on the market demand for those with these critical managerial skills.

Interestingly, for many years we have heard of the difficulties that companies have had in recruiting employees for a variety of low to middle income positions. If the market works as well as it should, these scarce employees should become more valuable and receive a relatively larger piece of the economic pie. Wage increases that result from such a more equitable sharing of the corporate pie should not be inflationary even without increases in productivity. Nonetheless, this is not what is happening in our economy.

To better understand the reason, we need only to look at the continuing crisis on our farms. The farm economy vividly demonstrates the problems regarding the relationship between productivity and income. In particular, farm income has continued to fall despite large gains in productivity. The government provides price supports and other interventions in a modest attempt to maintain stability. Unfortunately, the majority of federal farm subsidies go to 10 percent or less of the recipients, and the share received by large farms is reportedly likely to grow even further in the future. Thus, the small family farm continues to feel intense economic pressure despite continual strong increases in productivity.

Economists and politicians have often considered farm issues to be a special case. However, it may be that farming is actually an early warning system -- the canary in the mine -- for many problems that are inherent in our current socioeconomic system. The impact of productivity gains on the farm economy suggests that simple demands for productivity increases in the general economy may not produce the desired results.

Ravi Batra has compared these problems in agricultural income to the stagnation of real industrial wages. Despite similar increases in productivity, many workers in our industrial sector are suffering from problems that Batra describes as "agrification." That is, the problems facing industrial workers are beginning to resemble those that agricultural workers have faced for many years.

The economy asks them to produce more and more output in exchange for less and less real income. The declining quality of life for many workers as they work longer hours in an often futile attempt to maintain

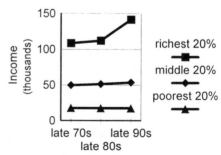

Figure 9 - Average Wisconsin family income (1999 $; see COWS, 2000b)

their incomes further compounds the problem. The Census Bureau noted in a recent report that among married couples with children, a majority now have both spouses working at least part time. Despite these efforts, the real family income for many has remained constant over the past twenty years as shown Fig. 9 for Wisconsin families.

Yet, our most affluent workers and managers continue to prosper even with uncertain gains in their personal productivity. In addition to generous compensation packages, we provide many other benefits to the affluent through a variety of governmental policies. These include such subsidies as tax deductions for mortgage interest on expensive homes, control of inflation for the benefit of creditors, government insurance for financial institutions used disproportionately by the wealthy, and loan guarantees and lucrative contracts for private businesses.

The affluent further benefit from the increasing tendency in our society to use the claim of equal treatment to justify policies that often disproportionately favor the wealthy. For more than thirty years, the federal government has steadily reduced the maximum tax rate resulting in a dramatic decrease in the taxes paid by high income taxpayers.

Younger taxpayers may find it hard to believe, but in 1965, the marginal tax rate for a couple with net income before exemptions (but after deductions) in excess of $400,000 was nearly 70%. In fact, the maximum rate was 70% in 1981 at the beginning of the Reagan administration. By the end of his administration, the maximum rate was only 33%. This puts complaints about current tax rates in a different light. It is true, according to a book by Alan Blinder, that despite these large rate reductions during the 1980s, the top 1% of families actually paid a 15% larger share as a group of total federal taxes in 1990 than in 1977. However, this seemingly contradictory result came about because this same group received a *53% increase* in their share of pretax income during the same period.

These same trends continue today some 20 years later. In early 2001, some federal tax cut proposals would have resulted in 43% of the tax cut going to the top 1% of the taxpayers who currently pay 21% of all federal taxes. This means they would have not only received by far the largest tax reductions (supposedly justified by the amount they pay), but double their relative share of current taxes (much harder to justify). The tax cut in the final bill contained similar provisions and provided a financial windfall for large corporations and upper income individuals. Later in the year, still more tax cut proposals emerged for the wealthy and large corporations.

Similar problems exist at the state level. For many years, Wisconsin has had a tax system that is highly regressive when considering the overall impact of property taxes, sales and excise taxes, and state income taxes. For this reason, lower income taxpayers pay a much higher percentage of their income in state and local taxes than the highest income taxpayers.

Flat or even regressive tax rate structures at the state and federal level reflect a reordering of the traditional priorities of our society. Regressive taxation contributes to a further widening of the gap between the wealthiest and poorest members of our society. In much the same manner, pressures continue for the elimination of the estate tax, which will almost exclusively benefit the extremely wealthy.

In addition to these trends, many governmental services have become increasingly funded through user fees, essentially another highly regressive form of taxation. For example, user fees increasingly support our public parks. In a reversal of long standing policy, the state Assembly in Wisconsin recently passed a recommendation to repeal existing state requirements and to allow municipalities and counties to charge their inhabitants for library services that they currently provide free of charge. There is also continuing movement at public schools towards increasing student fees. This includes charging students fees to participate in extracurricular activities such as athletics. Some fear such fees may turn sports teams into activities dominated by students from wealthier families.

Similarly, Wisconsin and other states continue to ask students to contribute an ever greater share of the cost of higher education. A recent report noted that nationally the cost of a college education for lower income families was much higher relative to family income than for upper income families. Lower income families reportedly paid an average of 62 percent of their real family income. In contrast, the wealthiest families paid only 7 percent of real family income. This report also noted that while this percentage has stayed constant over the past 28 years for the wealthiest families, it has increased by 20 percent for lower income families. Not a surprising result, in a world of increasing college costs, decreasing governmental support, and steady or falling income for most lower income families. Despite our calls for the poor to get more education, we continue to make it more difficult for them to pursue.

We do not have the same hesitation in helping large corporations or other more affluent members of society. During the past few years, a number of large bankruptcies have received considerable attention from the news media. Nonetheless, we should remember that throughout the nineties there have been other instances where the government has provided financial support or other assistance to large corporations that have financial problems. These corporations are so large and powerful that many of the characteristics of the free market no longer apply. We do not allow them to fail as readily as we would smaller corporations or businesses. The investors and corporate managers who invest or work in these large corporations continue to prosper despite the business problems that they encounter.

However, this same financial support is lacking when failure threatens smaller corporations and businesses. Small independent businesses come closer to reflecting the traditional characteristics of a free market economy. We allow them to fail and simply attribute it to the judgment of the market. Unable to externalize their costs and risks to the same extent as larger corporations, their survival becomes more uncertain. Their employees and owners, such as family farmers, small shopkeepers, independent professionals, and freelance workers, find it ever more difficult to avoid sliding down the economic ladder.

Just like the benefits received by mega-businesses, the already affluent continue to receive an ever growing number of additional subsidies and benefits from the government. No one seems overly concerned that these benefits or the existing wealth of the prosperous will adversely affect their work ethic. Many seem to consider huge increases in the compensation of the most wealthy and powerful members of our society justified and simply a natural result of the market system.

However, our system often questions similar benefits, subsidies, or minimal increases in income for the lowest income segments of our society. Some of the more affluent members of society even express concern over the negative impact of such increases on the work ethic of the poor. As a consequence, the inequality in income and wealth between the upper and lower income segments of our society continues to grow, creating economic distress for many people and social problems for our society.

The Dominance of the Business Paradigm

• Business decisions, language, and metaphors

Why do we collectively tolerate the growing dominance of the business paradigm and global corporations in our lives when it is responsible for so many problems and inequalities? We have allowed quantitative measures and business criteria to control our lives. In exchange, we presume that the economic gains for ourselves and our communities will outweigh the externalized costs of these businesses, including their social and environmental impacts.

Unfortunately, it is often difficult to determine even the direct financial impact of businesses on local communities, much less the indirect impact of externalized costs. Many businesses include their results in the financial reports of a large corporate owner. Others may transfer costs and liabilities to partnerships and other entities that they do not include in their financial statements. Pro forma financial results, intended for use in analyzing mergers and similar changes, provide another popular way to manage a company's perceived performance by labeling expenses as nonrecurring. In some cases, financial statements may be open to question due to increasing instances of financial manipulations, other accounting irregularities, and the growing tendency of mainstream corporations to pursue tax avoidance measures that the courts may later disallow.

The Enron bankruptcy in late 2001 brought a harsh reality to the accounting concerns raised by a variety of sources during the preceding months. As recently as October, 2001, Security and Exchange Commissioner Isaac Hunt gave a speech expressing his concerns related to improving the quality of the financial reporting system. Almost exactly one month later, the collapse of Enron's stock price and subsequent revelations of various issues with its financial reports emphasized the inherent weaknesses in current accounting procedures. Despite these problems, we continue to place our confidence in sometimes questionable financial data for evaluating our personal investments and planning the direction of our communities.

In addition to the excessive confidence we have placed on quantitative business measures for economic analyses, we have inappropriately expanded the application of these measures to many non-business aspects of our lives. Our communities include churches, schools, museums, art centers, recreation complexes, clubs, and many other non-business activities. Standard business accounting systems cannot evaluate their contributions to our lives and communities. The values and culture of these institutions are in retreat as business values and metaphors prevail in virtually all aspects of society.

In fact, our churches, schools, and other institutions now often accept the dominant language and values of business even in their own non-economic sphere of activity. They often refer to "the bottom line" despite the fact that they cannot evaluate many of their activities using "generally accepted accounting principles." Industry experts often encourage farmers to take an "agri-business" perspective rather than a more inclusive and traditional "agri-cultural" perspective that considers farming a way of life rather than simply another business. As mentioned previously, people in a wide range of relationships have become "customers" or "clients" versus the more accurate and traditional use of terms such as "students," "parishioners," or "patients." These various practices combine to reduce essentially all aspects of life to simply another form of business activity.

One of the most extreme examples of this tendency was a series of commercials run by a large financial company during the telecast of a recent golf tournament. The theme of these commercials was to reduce virtually all aspects of our lives to a series of business or financial propositions. The commentary suggested that a baseball game was actually a source of business for the ice cream truck, that a church was actually a site on the Web, and that a young child was actually a source of future earnings. While accurate in some limited sense, the attempt to reduce complex lives and cultural institutions to a simple business equation would seem inappropriate except in a world dominated by the business paradigm.

In addition to exporting of business language into various non-business areas of our lives, the world of business has co-opted language from these fields to serve business ends. In telecasts of the Olympics in 2000, one commercial referred to free access to the Internet as a "fundamental right," while another described the availability of computers with customized technology at a fair price as an "inalienable right." In both cases, businesses applied language usually reserved for important individual rights to relatively minor attributes of a product or service. This usage tends to trivialize these words and detract from the importance of the actual inalienable and fundamental rights described in the United States Declaration of Independence and Constitution.

• The roles of values

Today, there is considerable public debate over the role and standing of values in our society. Unfortunately, we live in a society in which economic materialism and the free market paradigm dominate nearly all aspects of our lives. There is an overemphasis on quantity rather than quality. We strive for high profits and low prices often at the expense of good jobs and quality products. We encourage our schools to teach for good test scores rather than to educate well-rounded future citizens capable of critical thinking. We look to our churches to reflect good business practices rather than influence our moral behavior.

One way to determine our values is to look at the pattern of our investments. At the University of Wisconsin in Madison, most buildings are quite functional in appearance. However, several years ago, the university constructed a new business school building that looks as much like a cathedral as a school. The exterior includes a tall spire on the roof and a huge colored glass window in the library that resembles a stained glass window. The floor plan is in the form of a cross with a soaring central interior space that suggests the nave. The new building dwarfs Luther Memorial Church, which is just a block away and was the former landmark structure in the neighborhood.

Although we continue to build some new university facilities, industrial parks for businesses have taken the place of college campuses in many communities as the primary source of community pride. Their broad expanses of beautiful landscaping dotted with the latest in architectural design reflect massive investment. It is rare to learn of the creation of a new college or university. On the other hand, a number of smaller schools in south central Wisconsin have closed in recent years including Milton College, a small liberal arts college; a private business college in Madison; and several parochial high schools in the Madison area.

Sometimes the contrasts created by our changing values are quite striking. A country club, not far from Madison, has a locker room, of all things, that also looks much like the nave of a large church. Huge wood beams line the towering cathedral ceiling and beautiful windows, not unlike leaded glass, line the walls. Thick red carpet covers the broad central aisle as well as side aisles filled with row upon row of wood lockers in place of pews. The room is spectacular and more impressive than many of the churches and cathedrals in the area.

What does it mean when our business schools and country club locker rooms look more like churches and our new churches often look like nothing much at all? Our money often expresses our values. We speak of basic values and the proper education of our children. And yet, we expend huge sums on new golf courses and business facilities, while schools, churches, and governments often operate under ever tighter financial restraints. We build our new churches with tight budgets and an emphasis on functionality. In those rare instances when we pass a referendum to construct a new school, the construction is usually basic with few frills. Government office buildings are typically plain, generic boxes.

Nonetheless, we always seem to find additional funding for a steady stream of new and ever more repressive prisons. Rather than seeking justice, we seek the maximum amount of retribution and punishment that the system will allow. As a result, we need ever more prisons as we create a permanent social and economic underclass. Strangely, the growing population of these prisons results more from the reclassification of crimes as well as changes in law enforcement, prosecution, and sentencing policies than any actual increase in criminal activity.

These judicial changes have had a very uneven effect on our society. We often focus our most intensive enforcement efforts on those areas where minorities and poor people live. Those arrested in these areas are less likely to be able to afford the costs of a strong legal defense. Furthermore, decisions by prosecutors concerning their cases are often subjective and may reflect the socioeconomic and cultural standing of the defendant. For example, the crime of dealing drugs usually leads to a much longer prison sentence than simply using drugs. In many cases, the facts might lend themselves to either interpretation of the suspect's behavior. The local prosecutor decides which charge to pursue. Statistically, minorities are more likely to receive more severe charges and resulting longer sentences. Combined with new truth-in-sentencing and no parole laws, the result is soaring prison populations in which minorities and lower income individuals are over-represented.

Wisconsin is a state proud of its agricultural heritage whose license plates still proclaim it America's Dairyland. However, in recent years, Wisconsin has had more people under the jurisdiction of its state Department of Corrections than farms. This non-parallel, but still amazing statistic is due to a *seven-fold increase* in those imprisoned, released on parole, or on probation from 1970 to 2000 combined with a moderate decline in the number of farms. In 1970, there were almost 10 times as many farms as people under corrections' supervision. Although partnerships or family corporations own some farms, the vast majority of Wisconsin farms are sole proprietorships. For this reason, there are probably now more people in Wisconsin under corrections' supervision than there are farmers.

A recent article noted that the proposed state budget in Wisconsin reduced a budget request by the state university system that would have allowed the enrollment of 8000 new students to an amount that will only support 600 new students. The same budget proposed the funding of three new prisons, the expansion of two existing prison facilities, and the creation of two facilities to teach job skills. We seem to prefer prisons and training over universities and education. Once again, our monetary choices reflect our values.

From the middle ages until the 19th century, the construction of great cathedrals and churches demonstrated the importance that we placed on religion. In the 19th and the early 20th century, great government buildings, inspirational monuments, and university campuses reflected an ultimate concern for democracy, freedom, and education. Classic examples include the Capitol in Washington, the University of Virginia in Charlottesville, the Statue of Liberty in New York, and our state capitol in Madison. Today, rather than churches, schools, or government buildings, our most impressive new facilities are corporate office buildings or arenas for business sponsored sports or entertainment events.

Corporate names on buildings often reflect this sponsorship and support. Historically, names of organizations or buildings have recognized great leaders or reflected an important core value of the community. Today, in many cases, they represent global corporations or business leaders. As such, they demonstrate the excessive pride that we have in the values, language, and successes of the business world, including our obsessive pursuit of efficiency and productivity.

In fact, the business paradigm has so penetrated our institutions that sale of naming rights has become a standard component for the funding of public facilities. Rather than recognizing the accomplishments or contributions of local individuals, we allow corporations to assign their names to our public stadiums, convention centers, and other facilities in exchange for an often rather modest flow of revenue. Once again, we allow the economic dimensions of the question to control our civic environment.

Corporate style image management also seems to have made inroads in the religious sector of our lives. For example, churches increasingly adopt names that are generic in nature and simply reflect some geographic feature or characteristic of the surrounding community. In contrast to the names of many older churches, these new names do not include any reference to the specific religious affiliation, historical teachings, or former leaders of these churches. A related trend that also parallels the corporate world is the growth of "mega-churches" with huge memberships and professional staffs to match. Churches in several major cities have well in excess of 10,000 members.

There are alternatives to our societal obsession with corporate models. I am a member of an older Lutheran church in Madison that has remained relatively small. Rather than aggressively pursuing growth, it has developed a niche ministry featuring alternative styles of worship, progressive social views, and a strong youth program. Inclusivity, diversity, experiences, and relationships are integral elements of its culture. Its organizational structure is informal. The church is a vibrant place that attracts members, not just from its immediate neighborhood, but from throughout the county with a higher percentage of active, committed members than many much larger churches. Rather than replicating opportunities available at countless other large churches in the area, it provides new alternatives and enhances religious diversity for the community.

From this simple example, we can see that the names on a membership list or the numbers on an accounting statement do not necessarily reflect success. We cannot reduce our loves, our relationships, and our lives to the calculus of economic calculations. Despite the pride and confidence we have in the power and language of business, life does not have a bottom line. Our lives are about more than a collection of numbers -- they are about more than winning and losing.

➢ Guidelines for economic justice

As Harvey Cox suggests, the market knows no limits and is ever-expanding. However, we live finite lives in a world of finite size for which market principles alone are not adequate. We need to move beyond allowing the market system and business paradigm to dominate virtually all of our discussions and decisions.

The language *of* business is the language *for* business. The other dimensions of our lives require a diversity of other languages. Our goal should be to create a healthy and meaningful life for all, rather than financial rewards for the few. To meet this goal, we need to:

- act on societal goals rather than simply react to market forces;

- include all people as active participants in our society and economy;

- find better ways to distribute our material wealth;

- enlarge our vision for the future;

- focus more on quality and less on quantity;

- build relationships as well as financial balance sheets;

- respond to human needs as much as economic productivity; and

- accept responsibility to create a more just and sustainable world.

The final chapter explores several different perspectives on the causes of the problems we are experiencing and suggests a variety of new approaches to their solution.

Toward the Future

A recent workshop in Appleton, Wisconsin, may have provided a glimpse of a more promising future. On a Friday night at the end of a long week, 25 people with a broad variety of backgrounds met to discuss economic issues related to corporate accountability and world trade. There were high school and college students, corporate professionals, employees from the service and manufacturing sectors, political activists, retired workers and managers, and others.

Following excellent presentations by a graduate student and a community leader from Madison, the group shared a light supper and continued the discussion for several hours. This led to the identification of many sources of additional information as well as opportunities for specific action steps. It was an inspiring evening filled with new ideas and attended by individuals who shared their common concerns about the direction of our economy.

* * *

Alternative Views of the Economy

As we have seen in the preceding chapters, aggressive global capitalism has generated intense competitive pressures and led to numerous corporate mergers. Corporate mergers concentrate economic power in a distant corporate headquarters that controls the economic future of local businesses and is the primary beneficiary of future corporate profits. Mergers disrupt the lives of the employees of the acquired business and their families. Some employees lose their jobs, while the remaining employees must deal with an unfamiliar and sometimes unappealing corporate culture. The former owners or shareholders receive substantial financial rewards, while many local employees and businesses often struggle to maintain their economic position. The local community faces a future filled with considerable uncertainty. It has fewer independent sources of employment, products, and services, as well as fewer potential customers for other businesses.

Ironically, it is becoming apparent that recent developments in our global economy are threatening not only the poorest members of society, but also middle and upper income individuals. Market declines and uncertainties brought about by concern over real and potential accounting irregularities endanger everyone's investments. Losses of employment, retirement accounts, and insurance benefits due to collapses like Enron affect employees and managers at all levels. Concerns over corporate lawsuits brought by foreign corporations under Chapter 11 of NAFTA limit our ability to take environmental actions against problems that endanger everyone's health.

In the past few years, a growing number of observers have published books expressing their concerns over these developments. These authors present a remarkably similar analysis of the nature of the problems and challenges that we are facing as a society. They express concern over the impact of aggressive capitalism and global corporations including the growing inequality of the distribution of income and wealth in our society. However, they often have differing perspectives on the fundamental causes of these problems and what alternatives we should consider.

Some place much of the blame on large scale capitalism as it has developed for well over 100 years. However, this perspective seems to understate the real benefits that our economic system has brought us. It also fails to acknowledge the negative impact of the substantial changes that have occurred in large scale capitalism over the past 20 years. The spread of deregulation and the global economy during this era represents a significant break with the past and coincides with the emergence of many of the problems discussed in this book.

It may well be important, as suggested by this book as well as many other writers, to give greater emphasis in our society to small businesses, alternative economic forms, renewable energy sources, more environmentally friendly forms of production, and the needs of local communities. However, it is difficult to see how we can fully meet our needs in such areas as food, energy, materials, transportation, and communications without significant use of giant enterprises. We will probably always need a mix of activities that includes many that are inherently very large scale, energy intensive, and environmentally troublesome. In these cases, societal oversight and regulation will be essential. The unregulated market is an imperfect system prone to many problems regardless of the size of the players. All companies regardless of size even in ideal markets require a certain amount of societal oversight.

Other writers, rather than emphasizing the impact of large corporations, have identified technological changes as primarily responsible for the problems so many people are experiencing in our so-called new economy. This view was perhaps more prevalent prior to the collapse of the dot-com bubble in the stock market and more realistic expectations for the Internet. Despite the apparent decline in the significance of these technological factors, concerns remain about the impact of global capitalism and corporate mergers on our lives and our communities.

Our current economy reflects economic and political decisions at least as much as the latest technological developments. We need to remember that we have lived with the impact of technological changes for over 200 years. What has changed over the past two decades is our broad embrace of the business paradigm, the supposed powers of deregulation, and the growth of global capitalism. We have adopted a willingness to restructure nearly all aspects of society in support of the business sector.

Proponents of the business paradigm present a false dichotomy between either accepting global capitalism with all its problems or turning our backs to progress. We need to remind them that society, through an evolving mix of regulations and controls, has reaped the benefits of business, trade, and technology for hundreds of years. During this period, it has also reserved the right to establish policies governing the types and methods of business that it would allow. We have endured the problems and shortcomings of unfettered global capitalism for only a few decades.

As a consequence, we need to find a way to make global corporations and the market economy more responsive to the needs of our society. Rather than reducing the problem to absolute acceptance or rejection of global capitalism and the new economy, we need to recognize the need to return to a more controlled and regulated form of capitalism. This alternative is an appropriate response to the problems of an economy and society increasingly dominated by the powerful and wealthy, while recognizing the real benefits of large scale businesses and global capitalism. The question is not primarily whether small or large businesses are better, but how we manage these businesses and control our economy to ensure the success of a diversity of economic players. For most of the 20th century, this seemed like a reasonable goal -- it is only quite recently that we have adopted economic policies that increasingly benefit an ever shrinking segment of our society.

The future success of our society demands that we reverse these trends and reorder our priorities. One of the barriers to this reordering is our use of the language of business and market economics to describe and evaluate virtually all aspects of modern life. We need to recognize that there are alternatives to this business paradigm. There is more to life than spreadsheets, financial analyses, and productivity gains. Many of the most profound and enjoyable aspects of life are economically unproductive and inefficient -- such as making music, writing a poem, painting a picture, or raising a child.

One of the most unfortunate outcomes of our obsession with the business paradigm is the way in which it has disempowered our society. We find ourselves basing our decisions on the results of cost/benefit analyses often using incomplete or inaccurate information. We give up our right to make our own decisions based on what we want or feel is the right thing to do. We must reclaim this right. Only in this way can we create a society that meets our needs instead of treating us like replaceable parts of some giant machine.

Proposals for Change

What can we do to regain control of the direction of our economy and society? There are many specific actions that we can take to produce a better balance between quantity and quality, between corporate power and individual rights, and between the desires of the wealthy and the needs of the poor. Some specific steps to consider include:

> ## *Diversity focus*

(1) performing an audit of the impact of corporate mergers and absentee owners on local communities;

(2) encouraging the growth of economic diversity;

(3) improving access to insurance and participation in economic decision-making processes for small businesses, volunteers, and nontraditional workers;

(4) enhancing local oversight of business activities;

(5) implementing economic impact reviews of major economic decisions;

> ## *Corporate focus*

(6) expanding the use of corporate advisory councils;

(7) applying adaptive management principles;

(8) reviewing the rights and obligations of corporations;

(9) broadening the rules for fiduciary responsibility;

(10) reforming the financial system;

> ## *Global focus*

(11) revising Chapter 11 of NAFTA, or its interpretation, to preserve the authority of local governments;

(12) preserving the virtues of comparative advantage;

(13) increasing global aid to help those poorer nations that are suffering from the effects of aggressive capitalism;

> ## *Local focus*

(14) increasing local aid to help communities suffering from the effects of mergers and economic relocations;

(15) taking political action to elect those representatives who will work for progressive change in our economy; and

(16) taking personal action to regain control of our lives and not allow the market to make our decisions for us.

The following sections will explore these proposals concerning our current economic problems in more detail.

> # Diversity focus

(1) Auditing the impact of mergers

A comprehensive audit of the short and long term effects of corporate mergers and absentee owners on businesses and the local community would help us to better understand how to proceed in the future. It is surprising how much resistance we often encounter to suggestions that we should evaluate the effects of corporate business decisions. For a society concerned with making employees in industry, government, and education accountable, we rarely obtain sufficient information to make our leaders accountable for their decisions. As usual, some may claim that the stock market makes these evaluations for us through the value of a company's stock. However, as we have seen, the market takes a short term, financial perspective and ignores many important factors in its evaluations.

We need to perform much broader reviews of the overall economic and social impacts of major corporate mergers on employees and their communities on both a short term and long term basis. Business leaders often tout the various anticipated benefits of a proposed merger. We deserve to know the actual effects of these mergers on businesses as well as the community.

(2) Encouraging economic diversity

As discussed previously, there are many steps that we can take to preserve and enhance economic diversity. Rather than continuing our pursuit of a monoculture economy comprised primarily of global corporations and mega-stores, we need to ensure a healthy economic garden filled with a diversity of businesses, organizations, and management styles.

One of the most important steps is to preserve the vitality of our small business sector. These include financial reforms such as new accounting practices that reflect the variety of direct and indirect benefits of small businesses to our local communities. We also need to reform our tax codes to recognize the local importance of small businesses, their inability to take advantage of many government programs, and their relatively low profitability. A more progressive business tax structure would strengthen many existing small businesses and encourage the formation of new businesses.

For a number of years, some companies have touted their "buy America" purchasing programs. We need to take similar steps to encourage and reward people both personally and collectively to "buy locally." The support of local retailers, suppliers, and distributors creates local economic and social strength within a community. We need to change our community development focus from retaining jobs to creating and retaining local businesses. Locally owned businesses generate benefits for the community that go far beyond the jobs and employment opportunities that they provide.

We also need to remember that there are many alternative organizational forms available to us to meet our economic and societal needs and increase the economic diversity of our communities. These include neighborhood associations, community farms, worker cooperatives, various nonprofit organizations, and professional associations. We need to think more imaginatively about how to encourage these alternative economic forms as well as our small business sector to perform new services and meet new needs.

A recent article provides an illustrative example of an innovative use of an existing non-corporate organization. The municipal water utility in Sun Prairie, Wisconsin, has begun providing broadband Internet access through a combination of fiber optic cable and radio transmitters located on its two water towers. The utility also provided the local school district with fiber optic service at an installation cost only one quarter of that in a bid by a private corporation.

The state association of telecommunications companies opposes this competition from public utilities, but thus far it has been unsuccessful in its attempt to obtain legislation banning the practice. A representative of the municipal power utilities noted that in the past some communities formed municipal power utilities when major power companies by-passed their community. In much the same way, broadband Internet service is now often difficult to obtain in some communities, and once again communities are using public utilities to fill the gap left by the private sector.

(3) Improving access and participation

Small business owners and employees, community volunteers, and nontraditional workers, such as those providing day care or health care at home, are invaluable members of our society and contribute to its economic well-being in many ways. Yet, in our increasingly corporate-centric world, they often have a very difficult time obtaining health and disability insurance. We need to provide more effective means for all members of the community to obtain these important insurance protections. Today, our system forces too many to choose between working for a large corporation, paying huge insurance premiums, or being uninsured.

We also need to develop new ways for these non-corporate workers to more fully participate in our economic decision-making processes. Too often, we focus the process on the views of the owners and managers of large businesses employing large numbers of employees. Individually each small business or nontraditional employment opportunity may employ only a few individuals, but collectively they represent an element of our society that deserves to have a greater voice when we consider proposed legislation or regulations.

(4) Enhancing local oversight

Regulations can play an important role in enabling local communities to review and influence local business activities. Zoning laws direct the use of privately owned land in ways that help meet the long range needs of the community. A recent court decision in New York State upheld the use of local zoning regulations to control developments that might adversely affect the local community. Strengthening such laws and encouraging their application throughout the country would help ensure that corporate developments create benefits for the local community.

There are other reviews that could also provide means to guide business decisions in a direction that is more beneficial for the local community. Environmental impact reviews, required for many large projects, often result in actions to protect sensitive areas or to restore comparable areas. Antitrust reviews to determine the impact of corporate mergers on competition, also required for large mergers, often result in the exclusion of certain assets from the merger. Applying these reviews to a broader range of decisions and requiring more local participation would further protect the local environment and economy.

There are other signs that local sensitivity to potential problems associated with commercial development is increasing. For example, the Madison Plan Commission recently rejected a proposal to construct a large discount store on a site near a wetland corridor. In addition to concern over the possible impact of run-off from a huge parking lot on the wetland, opposition focused on the large increase in traffic that the new store would generate.

In addition to thorough reviews of proposed developments, we also need to protect the interests of the local community through the development of appropriate controls on business ownership. There are precedents for laws that place some restraint on corporate ownership rights. On a global level, nations have passed foreign ownership laws to reduce the problems created by absentee owners and managers. For example, Brazil's constitution requires local ownership by individuals of both print and broadcast media. Unfortunately, due to the recent recession, intense competition, and the need for capital to invest in the latest technology, the Brazilian legislature is considering a constitutional amendment that would open media ownership to foreign investors. However, even with the proposed changes, Brazilians reportedly will still have majority control of the media companies and control of media content.

Some states in this country have passed laws that regulate the ability of large corporations to engage in farming in order to support family farming. Others have passed laws controlling the ownership of utilities that help retain local control. Following these precedents, new legislation might restrict outside ownership of local businesses without adequate compensation to the local community or require corporations to provide local investors or businesses with rights of first refusal before selling a local firm to outsiders.

In addition to legislation restricting the ownership rights of corporations, the corporate charter provides a means to identify more clearly the specific rights and obligations of the corporation. For example, the charter can require local participation in major corporate decisions. Society can also use the corporate charter to direct corporate behavior in other areas as well as to penalize inappropriate behavior through revision or, in extreme cases, revocation of the corporate charter.

There are two additional points to consider as we take steps to protect the economic health of our local communities and small businesses through regulatory activity. First, we need to recognize that our government enacts many laws and regulations aimed at the activities of large corporations that can create unreasonable burdens on small businesses. These laws and regulations, concerning taxes and many other areas, need to make more allowances for differences in company size. Global corporations with perhaps *a million times* more revenue and hundreds of thousands of employees are so much larger than the typical smaller business that it is unrealistic to expect one set of regulations to apply to all companies.

Second, we need to remember that our government often provides large businesses with special tax advantages and subsidies for the costs of infrastructure, training, and other areas, as discussed earlier. Small businesses rarely receive comparable treatment even though their collective impact can be quite large. We need to level the playing field between large corporations and small local businesses through more equitable use of financial incentives and supporting activities for small businesses that reflect the direct and indirect benefits of the small business sector to our local communities.

(5) Implementing economic impact reviews

In addition to existing reviews related to zoning, the environment, and antitrust considerations, there is a need for an overall economic impact review of all major economic proposals and decisions. This would include the review of corporate mergers for their economic impact on jobs, other businesses, community infrastructure, and other areas at the local, regional, and national level.

Such a review would be a natural extension of existing reviews and regulations. As mentioned before, we already require land use approvals, environmental impact statements, and antitrust reviews before we approve major development plans. Existing state and federal regulations address some of our environmental, health, and safety concerns. However, there are important impacts and concerns that these existing reviews or regulations do not address.

Recent concerns over vaccine shortages provide a good example. Until recently, there were two companies in the U.S. that produced the vaccine for tetanus and diphtheria. In January of 2001, one of these companies decided to stop making the vaccine. The remaining producer reported that it had inadequate time to increase production in response to the increased demand for its product. An economic impact review of the initial decision could have mandated a phased transition to allow sufficient time to bring new capacity into production.

Despite these types of problems, we do not require an overall evaluation of the economic impacts of major business and economic decisions. For a society, such as ours, that embraces the business or economic paradigm for most of its activities, it is not unreasonable to require a societal review of the economic impact of major business decisions. In addition to reducing problems like those discussed above regarding the production of vaccines, such a review would identify the direct and indirect costs for the community of the decision.

The overall community supported the activities of the business for many years. The local government, nonprofit agencies, churches, and schools served the company, its employees, and their families in a variety of ways. In turn, the business generated jobs and tax revenues for the community. Although this may provide an adequate return to the community for an ongoing business, this is not necessarily true when a business closes, moves, or changes owners.

Besides their annual profits, businesses can also create substantial unrealized value. The owners often must sell or close the business to realize this value. Although the taxing authorities may apply a capital gains tax on this gain, the sale most directly affects the local community. It suffers the greatest loss and must deal with many local economic costs associated with the change in ownership. The local community should recover some of its past and future costs associated with its support of the business from a share of this deferred gain. We can do this through more aggressive use of regulations and changes in taxation policy to mitigate the impact of corporate actions on the local community.

Monroe, Wisconsin, a small town south of Madison, has faced many of these types of problems as several cheese factories have closed over the past decade. At least one of these closures apparently occurred following the acquisition of the cheese factory by an outside company that simply did not need the additional production capacity.

The city of Monroe now has only about 10 remaining cheese plants. It had more than two dozen about 10 years ago. The local community must deal with a variety of potential problems related to the closures of these businesses including the loss of jobs, loss of tax base, vacant facilities, potential declines in school enrollments, and secondary impacts on other local businesses, churches, and so on.

In addition to the effects of cheese plant closings on the local community, the loss of small processing plants also harms family farms throughout the region. The remaining larger plants often do not want to collect milk from smaller producers. Thus, the small family farm has fewer alternatives available for the sale of its milk production and becomes more likely to go out of business. Consumers become more dependent on a smaller number of large producers.

Despite their impact on the local community of Monroe and the extended impact on family farms throughout the area, the local community had little or no input on these decisions and received no compensation for its investments in support of these plants and their employees for many years. Changes in regulations and taxation policies might help the situation, but an overall economic impact review is probably a better solution to resolving this inequitable treatment of the local community.

In the case of a proposed sale, merger, or plant closure, the consequences of an economic impact review might require various measures to mitigate its effects. These could include directing the owners to exclude portions of the business from the sale; to develop financing alternatives to encourage new local owners of part or all of the business or facility; to extend the time frame for the change; or to make a financial payment for the redevelopment of unneeded infrastructure, creation of new businesses, retraining or relocation of unneeded employees, and other direct and indirect costs.

Interestingly, legislators proposed a number of bills in the 1970s concerning plant closings, some of which included provisions for payments to local communities to assist in economic development activities. Unfortunately, Congress did not approve even these modest proposals, and the recent political climate has discouraged additional efforts by Congress in this area.

Nonetheless, there have been reports of several local efforts to require economic or environmental impact assessments of proposals related to mega-stores. For example, a recent article described the results of a required economic impact statement concerning the proposed expansion of a big box, retail store in Bozeman, Montana. This study led to a recommendation that the developers help fund additional advertising to promote existing stores as a way to mitigate the impact of the proposed expansion.

Similarly, the article also described the decision by a state environmental board to reject the proposed construction of a large store in Vermont due to the excessive costs it would generate for the public. Both cases provide optimism that in at least some communities, people are willing to take the steps necessary to regain control of their own economic future.

For the past 20 years, our society has focused its energy on deregulation, yet many people are beginning to recognize that there is a need for regulations that reflect our concerns for a more equitable and just society. Edward Luttwak describes in his book, *Turbo Capitalism,* the way in which our society too often serves the economy rather than having the economy serve our society. More general use of economic impact reviews would help provide increased control and oversight of the economy by the society that it should serve. It would help protect our economic security in much the same way as current reviews protect the environment, land use, and competition.

➢ Corporate focus

(6) Expanding the use of advisory councils

In the interim, while we debate and refine the preceding ideas, there are simpler steps that companies could take without great difficulty to open up the corporate decision making process to gain increased community involvement and support. One example is the increased use of advisory councils. Companies already use advisory councils areas such as technology and customer relations and could expand their use into other areas.

Advisory boards could serve as a useful resource when the board or senior management considers significant decisions for the company. These advisory boards could include representatives from employees, lower level managers, customers, suppliers, members of the local community, shareholders, and other important groups. Although it would require some administrative effort, such an approach would be straight forward to implement and provide an important way to obtain input from sources outside senior management.

Such groups could help ensure that corporate boards and officers have more complete and up-to-date information as they make decisions that will affect the entire community. Increased involvement of the greater community in the corporate decision making process could also help build acceptance and support for the final decision. Unfortunately, there is often considerable corporate resistance to even such seemingly modest proposals.

A recent shareholder proposal to DuPont suggested the formation of a committee with broad representation that would report to the corporate board on the community impact of plant closings. Such a report would help the board to develop alternatives to reduce the impact of such closings in the future.

Unfortunately, the board opposed the proposal stating that they felt they already had enough information. They felt that they already worked closely with local officials to minimize the impact of plant closings. Despite this claim, "minimize" does not suggest that there is no impact. In fact in some cases, these impacts can be substantial. A study of the type proposed could determine ways to further reduce or eliminate these problems.

It is likely that we will see little progress in these areas until corporate directors and officers take a fundamentally different view of their roles. They need to adopt the same team-oriented, collaborative spirit that companies stress with employees, customers, suppliers, and communities. They must develop a willingness to open up the decision making process and loosen their absolute control of the flow of information. In exchange, they would gain valuable insights and information from those outside the senior management group.

(7) Applying adaptive management principles

In a more general sense, we need to develop a greater understanding among our leaders and managers of the value of adaptive approaches to management and leadership. This includes creating a new balance between trust and control in order to develop more effective organizations. Building on the knowledge and experience of our employees, we can create organizations in which the emphasis is on action rather than analysis. We can empower our employees to use their individual initiative and make the numerous, small decisions that characterize responsive organizations.

Our companies, organizations, and society include many semi-independent units that are capable of self-organizing behavior when provided with a small number of rules and continuous feedback on their behavior. We need to develop a rich array of interfaces and interconnections between these units that enables learning to take place. With clearly stated overall goals and a relatively small number of simple rules, a flexible organization can function effectively and can adaptively learn how to better meet the needs of both the business and society. As discussed in greater detail in Chapter 4, such an organization more fully uses the inherent strengths of the company's employees.

(8) Reviewing corporate rights and obligations

It surprises some people to learn that our judicial system grants corporations the same legal rights and privileges as individuals. Corporations gained this legal standing through a simple statement affirming, without legal argument, the protections of the 14th amendment to the Constitution for a railroad corporation in a landmark 1886 U.S. Supreme Court decision. Corporations do not serve in the military, they do not serve on school boards, they do not serve prison terms for crimes they may commit. Nonetheless, through this Supreme Court decision, the law grants corporations free speech, due process, and equal protection rights just as for individuals.

The founders of our country, who pledged each other their lives and sacred honor, emphasized protecting our fundamental and inalienable rights. It is difficult to imagine them making such a pledge to protect the legal rights of corporations. They had sufficient concern for the maintenance of basic human rights for individuals in the face of an uncertain future that they attached the Bill of Rights to our Constitution. Today, individuals find themselves facing the growing power of a corporate world that is able to claim the same rights that we once reserved to individuals. In fact, through the use of policies such as mandatory arbitration agreements with employees and customers, corporations are able to assert even greater rights than real people.

David Korten in his book, *The Post-Corporate World,* has discussed the contradiction inherent in this extension of personhood to corporations -- namely, that you cannot own a person, but you can own a corporation. However, the effects on our views of individuals and their rights are perhaps even more disturbing. When we assign important human rights to legally created entities through judicial decisions, we trivialize these rights to nothing more than bullet points in a legal document that we can accept or deny, edit or remove.

As we extend the legal rights of individuals to inanimate legal entities, we reduce human beings to little more than legal entities that have no more rights than any other creation of our legal system. Visitors to our country often express surprise at the level of poverty and homelessness that they encounter amidst our seemingly endless wealth. The real needs of real people including adequate food, shelter, and medical care are often unmet. Human beings have a unique and fundamental claim to certain rights and freedoms that go beyond any legal contract. We need to return to the founding principles of our country that focused on protecting these rights of our people.

One way to approach this problem is to refocus our attention on the role of the corporate charter. People created the modern corporation. Today, we find ourselves enmeshed in a system in which the difference in power between individuals and corporations is creating problems throughout our society. We need to return to emphasizing the roles, rights, and obligations of the modern corporation through better use of the corporate charters that we use to bring these legal entities to life. We need to ensure that their rights are consistent with the obligations that we expect corporations to fulfill.

We should also reexamine the basis of the claim of personhood for the corporation. A reformulation of this claim should clearly distinguish between appropriate legal needs of corporations and the human rights of living individuals. People have inherent rights and needs that go far beyond what is necessary or desirable for legally created organizations.

(9) Broadening the rules for fiduciary responsibility

Due to their dominant role in our society, it is more critical than ever before that corporations reflect a connectedness with the broad needs of employees, suppliers, customers, and others in the community. There should be a deep commitment to something more than simply growth and financial success for the shareholders. In this way, they will be able to fulfill their general obligation to society as well as more effectively carry out their specific mission.

David Maybury-Lewis notes in *Millennium* that in some societies the economy functions to reflect important societal values such as the maintenance of relationships rather than providing a purely economic function. Corporations and their directors need to see their role as much broader than serving the needs of their shareholder owners.

Such a change in our view of the responsibilities of the directors and officers of a corporation will probably require modifications to existing securities regulations and broadening of our rules for fiduciary responsibility. Our current rules for fiduciary responsibility require that directors and officers give highest priority to the financial interest of the corporate shareholders. Under this standard, corporate attention can become intensely focused on short term financial results, often limited to simply the next few quarters. There is inadequate reflection on or concern for the long term impact of corporate decisions on even the financial results of the corporation, much less the greater community.

We need to expand our definition of fiduciary responsibility to include more responsibilities than simply short term financial gain for the shareholders. We need to recognize human rights within the community that have equal, if not greater standing, than the property rights of individual owners. To some, this proposition may appear controversial, but we must remember that the corporation is a creation of the community and its wealth is the direct result of community support and involvement.

This will lead to a significant change in corporate behavior. For example, there are many reasons why directors may consider the merger or sale of a company. These include competitive pressures, customer demands, legal pressures, lack of management personnel, financial needs, marketing problems, need for manufacturing capacity, and changes in technology. However, under current rules for fiduciary responsibility, a dominant consideration for virtually all mergers is money. In fact, at some point an offer to buy a company becomes so favorable to the shareholders that the directors are virtually unable to reject it even if they have concerns with its long term implications. Revised rules would allow directors to consider a broader range of long term needs of the business and its shareholders as well as other constituencies in the community.

(10) Reforming the financial system

For many years, the relative stability of our economy has been one of our fundamental, underlying assumptions. Those who grew up during the depression were under no such illusions. They experienced the impact of rapid and unpredictable economic change.

Recent events are bringing their concerns to life for a new generation. The fall of the Soviet Union in the early 1990s, although seen by many as a victory for the United States, was an early indicator of how rapidly change can occur in the post modern world in which we live. Over roughly the same period, the once celebrated Japanese economy faltered as their stock markets began a long, steady decline. Those of us in the United States should be under no illusion that we are immune to similar economic shocks.

In fact, the dot com stock market bubble broke in 2000, and with it, the hopes and dreams of investors, entrepreneurs, and employees. The subsequent economic recession brought further declines to stock markets and bankruptcy filings by numerous well known companies. Many employees lost substantial retirement savings along with their jobs in the collapse of Enron as well as a number of other major companies. In some of these cases, incomplete, misleading, or inaccurate information made it almost impossible for investors or employees to make informed decisions. We now are beginning to recognize that major economic dislocations are an ever-present danger.

Apart from the direct affect of these calamities on those personally involved, they create a larger problem for our society as a whole. Much of the long range economic planning of individuals as well as companies and the government assumes a reasonable level of stability and predictability in the financial world. We regularly borrow or lend large amounts of money for long periods of time. We purchase corporate bonds, long term annuity contracts, and long term care insurance policies from institutions that we assume will continue to function over the coming decades.

A prime question that we now face is how to restructure our financial system to insure the viability of these important long term contractual arrangements. It is essential that those responsible in business and government recognize the broad scope of the challenges that we are facing. A fundamental loss of confidence in the long term stability of our economic institutions could have a profound impact on our society. It is not sufficient to continue with business as usual.

We need to develop new safeguards to enhance the long term stability of our economic institutions. This may require a sophisticated combination of:

- new accounting practices with greater clarity and accuracy,

- new regulatory measures to provide improved control and monitoring of all types of corporations,

- new approaches to governmental insurance for a broader variety of institutions and investments,

- new forms of institutions structured to ensure greater long term stability, and

- greater emphasis on long term success over short term profitability.

These steps will help our society to regain control over our economy. They will enable us to move from a reactive mode to an active mode in meeting our societal goals.

However, despite the urgent need for reform in these areas, we must remember that financial reforms, improved accounting standards, and governmental regulations will never be adequate in themselves. It is also important to focus on the actual behavior that underlies corporate actions. As with adaptive management, a long list of detailed rules and regulations may not cover all situations. It more be equally important to articulate a few, broad rules that place the emphasis on protecting the rights of all members of the community rather than simply meeting overly specific requirements and regulations.

➢ Global focus

(11) Revising Chapter 11 of NAFTA

Recent free trade agreements appear to grant corporations rights that even go beyond those normally exercised by individuals. Under Chapter 11 of the North American Free Trade Agreement (NAFTA), foreign corporations in North America can sue a government for actions that the corporation believes are "tantamount to expropriation."

This means that U.S. corporations can file lawsuits based on governmental actions against either Canada or Mexico. Similarly, Canadian and Mexican corporations can file lawsuits against the the U.S. and Mexican or Canadian governments, respectively, under NAFTA. The Free Trade Area of the

Americas (FTAA) legislation proposes similar rights for foreign corporations in countries throughout the Americas.

Representatives negotiating these treaties presumably approved these provisions as protections against seizures or other unreasonable actions by governments against foreign corporations. Today, corporate lawyers are using this broad language as the basis for lawsuits whenever they believe actions such as environmental regulations cause an economic loss to their corporations. Ironically, these efforts to protect corporations from environmental regulations and costs come at a time when the growth of large corporate facilities increases the likelihood of environmental crises.

In addition, it is possible that corporations may file future actions based on other forms of governmental actions concerning a broad range of issues including land use policies, energy policies, and procurement criteria. This provision of NAFTA threatens nearly all governmental actions attempting to regulate society for the common good that involve a certain amount of expense and loss of freedom. In fact, it appears that Chapter 11 of NAFTA threatens the ability of government to carry out its basic functions. The closed tribunals that hear these lawsuits under the treaty are beyond the range of normal public scrutiny and further compound the problem.

As a result of these problems and challenges to our own representative government, we need to:

- either renegotiate, revise, or modify the interpretation of Chapter 11 of NAFTA;

- insure that future trade agreements including the FTAA proposal do not contain similar language;

- open up the tribunal process to public observation and participation;

- open up participation in World Economic Forums to a broader range of constituencies;

- make globalization discussions and trade negotiations more responsive to the democratic process; and

- recognize basic human rights in all future trade agreements much like the Bill of Rights in the U.S. Constitution.

(12) Preserving comparative advantage

The economic doctrine of comparative advantage suggests that free trade without restrictions will be to everyone's benefit even for countries that are less productive in all areas. The doctrine presumes that these less productive nations will naturally gravitate to producing those goods in which their relative disadvantage in productivity is least. That is, they will produce those goods in which they have a comparative advantage. Their efforts will enable other countries to focus their efforts on those areas in which they are most productive. Overall global production will increase, and all nations will benefit.

In the new world of global capitalism, it is becoming more difficult for many countries or their residents to direct the use of their productive resources. In countries with weak economies and relatively low productivity, outside corporate owners often control many of the productive resources of the nation. There is no need for these absentee owners to follow the logic of the theory of comparative advantage and to continue to operate an inefficient plant.

As discussed previously, according to some reports, this phenomena is at least partially responsible for the economic problems that Argentina is currently experiencing. If an outside corporation owns a plant in Argentina that is less productive than its plants in other countries, it may simply choose to close the plant. A new principle of absolute advantage is replacing the principle of comparative advantage. The foreign owner is under no obligation to find an alternate use for this plant and its employees. The decisions made by these foreign owners to allow local plants to lie idle while they operate more productive plants elsewhere has contributed to massive unemployment. Ironically, at the urging of the leading industrialized powers, Argentina pursued a policy of privatization and deregulation during the 1990s which has coincided with increased foreign ownership of economic assets, reduced growth, and its current financial problems.

These developments in Argentina may also be a warning for our own country. Foreign investment in manufacturing facilities in the United States has significantly increased in recent years. Some of the most highly publicized have been decisions by foreign automotive corporations to construct huge new assembly plants in the U.S. Although many states often compete for the jobs in these plants, the high paying headquarters jobs still remain overseas along with the corporate profits and the ultimate corporate decision making power. In addition, the news articles announcing the chosen locations of these plants often stress the financial incentives that the host state will provide as well as the relatively low cost, non union labor that is available.

The impact of out-of-state or foreign owners is evident in Wisconsin. Increasingly, absentee corporate owners control the economic resources of the state. They are free to close production facilities in Wisconsin whenever they wish without regard to the impact of these closures on the local economy. Decisions to close or reduce Wisconsin operations by foreign, out-of-state or non-local owners have occurred in some of the most important sectors of its economy including breweries, food processing plants, and manufacturing facilities.

If Wisconsin or local investors and managers owned and managed these plants, they would be more likely to remain in operation even if they were not as productive as facilities outside the state. Employees might earn lower wages and investors might receive less profit, but the employees, investors, and managers would jointly recognize the need for jobs and some financial return on their fixed investment.

We need to find innovative ways for the local community to reassert collective oversight of the productive assets in their community. As suggested earlier, this may require restrictions on absentee ownership or local options to purchase, lease, or borrow idle or underutilized facilities. It may require regulations concerning the need for local financing and the use of local suppliers. We must balance the benefits of free trade with the need to maintain viable local economies throughout the world that can provide the necessities of daily life.

(13) Increasing global aid

As described above, the impact of globalization has been severe in many nations, often exacerbated by ill-advised suggestions that they privatize and deregulate their economies. As the wealthy, economic leader of the world, the United States needs to dramatically increase its foreign aid to these needy countries.

In 1970, the United Nations recommended that wealthy countries like the United States give 0.7% of their Gross Domestic Product (GDP) as foreign aid to poorer countries. A recent list in *The Economist* showed that in 1999 the United States gave 0.1% of its GDP in foreign aid -- by far the lowest percentage of the major industrialized nations on the list. Denmark (1.01% of its GDP), Norway (0.91%), the Netherlands (0.79%), and Sweden (0.70%) were at the top of the list. Many other countries gave 2-3 times as large a percentage of their GDP as the United States. Modest increases in foreign aid would help others and contribute much more to our national security than comparable increases in military spending.

➤ Local focus

(14) Increasing local aid

In addition to increased foreign aid, we must recognize that private business decisions and market forces will often be at odds with the needs of local communities. We must be willing to take collective action to help local communities as they pass through the painful transitions that are common in the new global economy. We cannot simply sit back and hope that traditional market forces will respond quickly and effectively to meet their needs.

This will require action by the government, nonprofit organizations, businesses, and individuals to redirect resources at the local level to meet human needs. It may include direct financial aid to individuals, local institutions, and local government; the maintenance or modification of existing infrastructure; and the development of new businesses and jobs.

This is not a radical or new idea. Collective action for the common good permeates much of our country's history. It is only recently that the focus of our society has shifted from the power of collective action to an obsession with the rights of individual property owners. We need to again see ourselves as temporary stewards of our property and resources. It is our responsibility to work with others to ensure that we use our resources to build stronger local communities.

(15) Taking political action

Ultimately, those of us with a desire to change the way in which our society sets its priorities and structures its economy need to become more directly involved in the political process. Many of the preceding proposals will require state and federal legislatures to pass new laws and agencies to implement new regulations. Current legislation and regulations either ignore many of these issues or do not go far enough to ensure a just and fair playing field for all individuals, communities, and businesses.

For example, the American Booksellers Association, a trade association representing small, independent bookstores, has had an ongoing struggle with large bookstore chains and publishers over practices that it feels undermine small bookstores. It has reportedly been difficult to obtain relief in the courts from these practices under current laws. Their task would be easier if new legislation and regulations gave increased recognition to the special needs and contributions of small businesses.

In another illustration of the problem, it was support for deregulation and their own agenda for the media in the 1990s that encouraged legislators to pass laws allowing the concentration of ownership of television and radio broadcasting discussed earlier. Similarly, it will now take new legislation to reverse these trends and reclaim the airwaves as a diversified medium of discussion and entertainment. Fortunately, there is some indication that such changes may in fact occur. A recent article suggested that there is now legislative movement to review and possibly modify the legislative that enabled these huge consolidations to occur.

In order to pass this type of legislation, we will need to identify and elect political leaders who are willing to move beyond old clichés regarding the free market and demonstrate leadership in developing new approaches to global capitalism. We need to abandon the black and white thinking that permeates our political system and that makes any criticism of free markets and aggressive capitalism unacceptable. Perhaps, the recent slide in the markets as well as the collapse of a number of major companies will embolden us to regain political control of our own economy.

Some people are working hard for renewal within existing party structures, while others see the need for a new political party. In either case, the recent presidential election demonstrates that significant differences exist between various candidates and their programs. Despite the suggestions of some to the contrary, this election has resulted in a Bush administration with a very different set of priorities than those supported by Al Gore or Ralph Nader. These priorities have directed the administration's appointments, proposed legislation, regulatory actions, and public rhetoric. Those with different priorities should find strong incentive to work for their candidates as well as reform of our election practices including campaign finance reform.

Recent developments suggest that we may find growing political support for these reforms as well as reforms in our oversight of the economy. In addition to recent concerns over the collapse of several major corporations, people are beginning to recognize that those of us in the developed world are facing many of the same problems that developing countries have had to contend with for many years. A documentary movie, *Life and Debt,* presented at a recent fair trade conference in Madison, demonstrated the significant parallels between the challenges that we face in Wisconsin and those in many developing countries.

The movie included the story of how the import of low cost milk powder has severely affected local milk production on the island of Jamaica. Due to a combination of factors, including advanced technology, highly productive land, genetically superior cows, and government subsidies, high volume producers in developed nations can deliver powdered milk into Jamaica at prices that are significantly lower than local producers. As a result, local farmers have lost their jobs and local facilities lie idle. Local consumers may pay lower prices at least in the short term, but have less control of their food supply. Without local production, they are now dependent on global corporations which can raise prices or cut off supply without warning. In addition, the milk may contain hormones and other chemicals that some consumers may prefer to avoid.

This story is not exceptional. Recent reports described the decline of local milk production in Sri Lanka over the past 20 years. Beginning in 1981, the government pursued a policy of deregulation and privatization that led to a consolidation of the dairy industry. In April, 2001, the International Monetary Fund (IMF) placed loan conditions that led to currency devaluation and increases in the tax on milk. Meanwhile, the price of a packet of milk has increased at an average annual rate of more than *12% per year* from 1977 to 2001. The cost of just the ten packets of milk typically required each month for a single child now exceeds the *total* monthly income of an average, poor family. In response to these severe problems, local reform movements have campaigned for the elimination of the tax on milk, the elimination of advertising for dairy products, the use of packaging alternatives, increased education on nutrition and breast feeding, and the revival of the local dairy industry.

Much like these problems in developing nations, Wisconsin's dairy industry has suffered under strong competition from dairy producers in other states who operate huge production facilities, sometimes with thousands of cows. As discussed previously, production facilities with huge numbers of animals confined at high densities can pose potential threats to the environment, animal health, and continuity of supply. For years, the owners of large dairy production plants in distant states have also benefited from an outmoded pricing system in which producers received a minimum milk price that increased with their distance from Eau Claire, Wisconsin.

The new farm bill recently passed by the House and Senate will equalize milk prices across the nation and introduce federal subsidies for dairy farmers. However, many believe that these subsidies, which will apply only to the first 2.4 million pounds of milk produced annually (equal to that produced by about 140 cows; a relatively large number for many family farms in

Wisconsin), will encourage overproduction. Smaller producers, who often have 50-100 cows, may decide to increase the size of their herds to gain the maximum subsidy. In addition, a recent article noted that there are loopholes available in the new farm bill that may enable large producers to receive subsidies beyond the supposed limits in the bill.

Larger producers may also expand production to maximize use of their investments in a period of falling prices. Consequently, the beneficial effects of the subsidies for smaller farms may be more than offset in a few years by falling prices. These declining prices may further eliminate smaller producers with ultimately harmful effects for consumers. Due to the complicated relationship of these various factors, opposition to the new farm bill may have included those who oppose subsidies for relatively large producers, fear the long term effects of overproduction, or oppose subsidies as contrary to free and open markets.

Whatever perspective one might take, the role of Wisconsin's dairy industry in the state's economy has gradually decreased. Family farms have declined along with many rural communities. Industry experts have often encouraged the remaining farmers to adopt new technologies and expand, perhaps beyond their desires, in order to remain competitive. Much like farmers in developing countries, they have become dependent on outside corporations for proprietary seeds, fertilizers, hormones, antibiotics, and other agricultural chemicals that are expensive to purchase and whose long term effects on the land, animals, produce, and people may be undesirable.

Due to these economic pressures, many Wisconsin dairy farmers now pursue alternative jobs on either a part time or full time basis to supplement or replace their farm income. In many cases, they take manufacturing jobs where the work is physically repetitive and the wages modest.

In much the same way, displaced agricultural workers in developing countries, including Jamaica, often seek jobs at assembly plants in Free Trade Zones, known as "maquillas," where they work under highly controlled, difficult conditions for very low wages, assembling clothing or other products for sale in developed nations. In some cases, workers are able to obtain jobs in manufacturing plants that are outside of the Free Trade Zones, but still owned by large foreign corporations.

Like non-locally owned plants in Wisconsin, these manufacturing jobs provide much needed jobs in an economy that is losing its agricultural base, but wages are modest and the profits flow to outside owners. In addition, in order to obtain the corporate investment that provides these jobs, developing nations as well as many farm states, particularly in the Midwest and South, offer substantial benefits in the form of favorable tax treatment or outright grants for development of needed infrastructure. Corporate managers often cite the availability of low cost labor, lack of unions, and limited governmental interference when they announce the location of a new plant. Despite these incentives and concessions, there is often no guarantee that the plant will be more than a temporary employer in the local community. When this occurs, without either a manufacturing or agricultural base, the economic future is grim.

From the above discussion, it is clear that workers in Wisconsin and many other states are facing many of the same problems that are facing workers in developing nations. Interestingly, it is also becoming clear that these problems are also spreading across all economic classes. We can no longer afford to ignore these issues by pretending that they only apply to poor people in developing nations. Today, these issues are also affecting the lives of middle income and even upper middle income workers in wealthy countries like the United States.

For these reasons, those struggling in developing countries may find that there is more support for their struggles than they might expect in developed countries. In addition, those of us confronting these issues in developed countries may find that we have much to learn from those in developing countries who have been dealing with these problems for a much longer time. Thus, there are powerful reasons for people in all nations to work and learn together as they develop new approaches to creating a more humane and sustainable economy.

(16) Taking personal action

In the meantime, there is a viable alternative that many of us can pursue on our own. An increasing number of people are beginning to recognize that they can retake control of their economic lives. The demands of short term returns or fiduciary responsibility do not constrain our decisions regarding our personal economic lives.

We can conduct our own personal economic impact review when we face important decisions regarding our work and investments. We can make our decisions in such a way as to meet our needs and the needs of those around us without regard to the short term returns on our investments or impact on our income. We can follow our own dreams and values. We can acknowledge our own strengths and abilities. We can become more actively responsible for our own lives.

It is not always easy to take a more active role in our lives and communities. The modern world prefers a passive stance reflected in the passive voice used in professional or corporate papers and reports. The professional world prefers its implied objectivity. The corporate world likes its inherent ambiguity.

The passive voice also fits very well in the new world of global capitalism, seemingly dominated more by systems than individuals. In such a world, people don't move things -- things are relocated. Engineers don't create designs -- designs are developed. Sales personnel don't sell products -- products are sold. People don't make mistakes -- mistakes are attributed to computer errors. There is often no criticism or blame or praise; there is only the system.

For example, a recent inquiry reported that engineers had miscalculated the Doppler shift of the signal from a probe scheduled to enter the atmosphere of Titan, one of Saturn's moons, in 2005. Due to this error, technicians installed an incorrect component in the orbiting spacecraft that they expected to receive the probe's signal and relay it to Earth. Fortunately, engineers were able to develop an ingenious solution that appears to have solved the problem. However, the inquiry into the mistake assigned no blame for the error to any individual or organization. Rather, it concluded that the system was responsible for the error.

Apparently, for some people at least, we live in a world where only systems make mistakes. Their preference for the passive voice and reluctance to assign blame may stem from fear of the consequences of making mistakes. We live in a legalistic society that is only too ready to take retribution and to administer punishments to those who break its rules. For this reason, people may seek refuge in the anonymity of the passive voice in which there is no one to blame.

Alternatively, many people believe that only systems achieve successes. This attitude allows corporate management to devalue individual skills and experience, acting as if any employee is readily replaceable and that most anybody can fill most any position. It is the ultimate manifestation of the disempowerment discussed in this book. Interestingly, this attitude diminishes at the highest levels of the corporation where directors often act as if the most senior executives are truly irreplaceable and reward them with compensation packages that reflect this common, if also inaccurate, perception.

Our personal use of the passive voice also reflects our feelings of powerlessness in the face of the corporate system. We are all affected by numerous decisions made for us by others that we cannot control or influence. The passive voice helps us to hide our true feelings.

Unfortunately, a variety of social and technological trends have further undermined our self-confidence and created a more passive orientation to our lives. For example, in the 1960s, many owners maintained their own automobiles. They performed routine maintenance, did their own tune-ups, and made a variety of repairs. Today, the demands of the workplace combined with two wage earners in many families limit the amount of time available for these activities. In addition, cars have become so complex due to computers, emissions controls, and various accessories that it is much less practical to service your own car.

As a result, we have become more dependent on professional mechanics to perform tasks we formerly did ourselves.

Similarly, those of us growing up in the 1950s and 1960s may recall enjoyable experiences with chemistry sets, model airplanes, or electronics kits. Some of us performed experiments described in *Scientific American* or *Popular Electronics* magazines. Others designed and constructed model airplanes with miniature gasoline engines. Some of us had our own ham radio equipment. These experiences with designing, building, and soldering things with our own hands gave us a feeling of empowerment and control over our environment. Today, we purchase our computers and cell phones like any other appliance. We wait for the Internet connection to be completed for us. We send equipment away for repairs or simply discard it and replace it with the newest model.

We live in a world that encourages us to wait for some commercial company to tell us about our latest needs and offer products to meet them. We need to take a more active role in our lives. We need to find our active voices -- both figuratively and literally. Our active voice allows us to get in touch with our true feelings. It enables us to act more assertively about the problems that we encounter and regain control of our own lives.

- As employees, we can choose our jobs and careers based on our personal callings as much as economic gain. We can pursue career paths that enable us to develop our potential and to serve important needs of our society. We can seek jobs with companies and organizations that have core values, an organizational culture, and a management style that reflect our own values and preferences.

- As managers, our decisions can reflect fundamental values such as sustainability, fairness, and justice. We can insist on ethical business practices in our relationships with employees, suppliers, investors, and competitors. We can support and encourage local businesses.

- As business owners, we can establish corporate policies that encourage long term results and responsible management. We can work to strengthen the local economy and to retain local ownership of our businesses.

- As individual investors, we can invest in socially responsible corporations and take a long term perspective.

- As entrepreneurs, we can start businesses to enhance the economic strength and diversity of our local communities. We can search for opportunities to meet important unmet societal needs rather than simply look for the easiest way to get rich.

- As consumers, we can move beyond simply looking for the lowest prices and make environmental, energy, and social concerns an imperative. This means using energy efficient appliances, reducing and consolidating our travel, and patronizing local merchants. Good shopping does not mean paying a low price, but paying a fair price. Wherever and whenever possible, we can purchase products from local producers, community farms, or on the fair trade market.

We need to make economic and social justice part of all that we do. Political action is important, but it must begin with the way in which we live our lives and make our personal business decisions.

Restoring Our Vision for the Future

In the new world of aggressive global capitalism, everyone and everything is vulnerable to ongoing change and reorganization. Nothing seems to endure. Corporations buy, sell, merge, rename, reorganize, and declare bankruptcy on a regular basis. New management arrives and departs through the proverbial revolving door. Stock prices and retirement accounts go from boom to bust in a matter of weeks or even days. If this seems like hyperbole, look up some of the recent declines in the stock market, particularly for telecommunications, energy, and technology related companies.

Perhaps the short term thinking that dominates corporate decision making shouldn't surprise us -- for many managers and companies, there literally is no long term future. In the meantime, local communities and employees must find a way to survive. We, as well as our children and grandchildren, will live with the long term consequences of business decisions, often made by the few for the many, long after the corporations themselves may have disappeared.

The modern corporation has made many substantial, beneficial contributions to our lives. We need to develop innovative ways to maintain its strengths while increasing its accountability to society for its decisions. Reestablishing the proper role of government oversight is necessary to provide a counterbalance to the ever growing power of global corporations. In order for democracy and free markets to survive, we must regain control of our economy from those who would prefer the concentration of political and economic power in the hands of the few.

Many would present this issue as a false dichotomy between governmental control and socialist thinking on the one hand versus private ownership and free market capitalism on the other. Whatever the theoretical advantages of free and open markets, it is clear that in real world, market consolidations and corporate mergers continue to move us ever further from this theoretical ideal. In the name of free market capitalism, we are allowing global corporations to threaten and in some cases destroy many small businesses. Ironically, the relationships of these small businesses with their customers, suppliers, and competitors most nearly approximate the free market ideal that we claim to desire.

We have a responsibility for the world we leave future generations. This means we must make our economic system more responsive to the long term needs of our communities. Our vision for the future must extend beyond the business paradigm. We need to find new words to express our hopes and dreams more effectively than the language of business. We need to renew our existing institutions and create new institutions to meet societal needs. Our success in building a strong society and economy for the long term future depends on our ability to:

- reexamine our fundamental values and priorities;

- learn from the experiences of our predecessors;

- consider the needs and desires of future generations;

- balance local issues with global concerns;

- encourage a more diverse economic system;

- create a more inclusive society;

- move from controlling to caring;

- recognize that life is about more than productivity;

- find new language to express our personal and societal goals and aspirations;

- seek peace and justice through our actions and decisions;

- take personal and collective responsibility to build a better world.

We can begin by letting go. Various writers including the theologian, Matthew Fox and, more recently, the poet, Joyce Rupp, have suggested that the process of emptying is part of life or rebirth. Only by letting go will we be able to remember where we have been and to recognize where we should be going. We need to let go of our faith in the market system to make all of our decisions, to move beyond our obsession with the business paradigm, and to recognize that life is more than the bottom line -- more than a business decision.

We need to take active steps to make real our claim that this is the land of opportunity for all. We must invest more in our people and communities. This means less money for country clubs and prisons -- and more money for schools and children. This means less concern for the high taxes of the wealthier members of society -- and more concern for the low incomes of the poorer members of society.

Our society is not a collection of parts in a giant machine. It is a giant tapestry of lives and organizations with a variety of colors, textures, and patterns. The removal or neglect of any of the threads of the tapestry can destroy the integrity of the whole. In order to restore the fabric of our communities, we must seek a rebirth of our society based on human needs rather than the demands of the economy. We need to help all people develop their unique potential. We need to move beyond methods and systems, and focus on individual strengths and identity. We must change the way in which we make our decisions. We must move from making business decisions to making people decisions.

✍ Chapter Notes and References ✍

Selected acronyms:

ABA   American Booksellers Association
AHRC   Asian Human Rights Commission
ALRC   Asian Legal Resources Center
CEO   Chief Executive Officer;
COWS   Center on Wisconsin Strategy;
CPS   Current Population Survey;
DMCA   Digital Millennium Copyright Act;
FTAA   Free Trade Area of the Americas;
IEEE   Institute of Electrical and Electronics Engineers;
LCA   Lutheran Church in America;
MABC   Madison Area Business Consultants
NAFTA North American Free Trade Agreement;
NIST   National Institute of Standards and Technology;
PDP   Professional Data Processing (Nelson unit);
SAE   Society of Automotive Engineers;
TQM   Total Quality Management;
UW   University of Wisconsin;
WCC   Wisconsin Conference of Churches.

Preface

p. 5: on business rankings, see Levering, et al., 1993; Ivey, 2002b.

Chapter 1. Mergers in Wisconsin

p. 10: early history of Nelson, see *Nelson,* 1989.
p. 15: technical background on active sound control, see Widrow, 1985;
       Eriksson, 1985; 1992; 1996; Kuo, et al., 1996.
p. 16: formation and history of Digisonix, see Seppa, 1992; Silver,
       1992a; Eriksson, et al., 1994.
p. 16: active sound control, *New York Times,* see Broad, 1987; *Time,*
       see Elmer-Dewitt, 1989; *Science,* see Alper, 1991; also see
       Allman, 1991.
p. 16: Digisonix growth and Ford program, see Seppa, 1992;
       Digisonix, 1992a; 1992b; J. Riddle, 1992; *The Capitol Times,*
       1992.
p. 16: Digisonix program with Lord Corporation, see *Wisconsin State
       Journal,* 1994; Maloney, 1994; Nairn, 1994.

p. 19: Nelson history published for 50th anniversary, see *Nelson,* 1989.

p. 20: information on the sale of Nelson, see *Nelson,* 1997; *Cummins,* 1997a; 1997b.

p. 20: published articles on the sale of Nelson, see Brezonick, 1998; Ivey, 1997a, 1997b; Newman, 1997a; 1997b; Savage, 1997.

p. 23: Mattel purchase of Pleasant Company, see Gribble, 1998.

p. 23: StarBanc purchase of Firstar, see Causey, 1998.

p. 23: Firstar merger with U.S. Bancorp, see Dickey, 2000; Ivey; 2000; Newman, 2000c.

p. 24: GE purchase of Lunar, see Barrett, 2000b.

p. 24: Target purchase of Rowley-Schlimgen, see Newman, 2000b.

p. 24: Sherwin-Williams purchase of Mautz, see Ivey, 2001; Ivey, 2002a.

p. 24: Sears purchase of Lands' End, see Richgels, 2002; *The Capital Times,* 2002c.

p. 25: Wisconsin's largest corporations and data on comparable states, see *Fortune,* 2002; *Forbes,* 2002; Milfred, 2000b; Farnham, 1989.

p. 28: use of meetings in larger organizations, see Carlton, 1997.

p. 29: standardized approaches of large corporations, see Carlton, 1997.

p. 29: delegation, see Galbraith, 1992a.

p. 31: on mergers and culture, see Armour, 2000; Lohr, 2001; Mateja, 1999; *The Capital Times,* 2000b; Spain, 2001; Suhr, 2001.

p. 31: importance of roles in personal work, see Bellman, 1990.

p. 32: comments on corporate lifestyle, see Hammer, 1996b; Uchitelle, 2000; Fraser, 2000; Andresky, 2001; Wineke, 2001b.

p. 32: on Wisconsin wages, see *COWS,* 2000a, 2000b; 2001.

Chapter 2. Power and the Corporation

p. 35: on corporate power, see Drucker, 1973; 1989; Tarrant, 1976.

p. 36: on corporate directors, see Beaver, 1999; White, 2000; Luttwak, 1999.

p. 36: selection of board, see Galbraith, 1992b; 1994a; Eriksson, 2002.

p. 36: on relationship between directors and CEOs, see Greising, 2002a.

p. 38: on changes in corporate governance, see Teitelman, 2002.

p. 39: on loss of headquarters, see Milfred, 2000b; Wineke, 2001a; Bluestone, et al., 1982a; Luttwak, 1993a.

p. 40: on corporate headquarters and wages, see Milfred, 2000b.

p. 41: comparative advantage, see Samuelson, 1964; Luttwak, 1993b.

p. 41: on economy in Argentina, see Smith, 2001; Rohter, 2002.

p. 42: the underground as metaphor for our technological society, see Williams, 1990; K. Eriksson, 1999;

p. 43: on literary allusions to underground, see Nin, 1948; Updike, 1981; Paz, 1991a.

p. 45: role of nature, see Williams, 1990; K. Eriksson, 1999.

p. 46: role of history, see Patton, 2000; Zinn, 1980.

p. 46: on the loss of nature and historicity; see Colás, 1994.

p. 48: the here and now, see Brand, 1999; Paz, 1991b.

p. 48: on New Balance shoes, see Harkavy, 2002.

p. 52: new store, see Shaw, 2000; Knaapen, 2000a; 2000b.

p. 52: 2nd store, see Fitzgerald, 2000a; 2000b; Knaapen, 2000c.

p. 53: effects of large stores on business districts, see Korten, 1999a.

p. 53: on corporations and externalized costs, see Korten, 1995; 1997; 1999b; Luttwak, 1999a; Greene, 2001.

p. 54: local resistance to proposed store, see Erickson, 2001.

p. 55: seasonal workers, see Milam, 2000.

p. 55: effects of mandated quality programs, see Uzumeri, 1998

p. 57: NAFTA and RTAA, see Seligman, 2001; Sierra Club, 2000; *Public Citizen,* 2000; *Global Exchange,* 2000; Longworth, 2001; Nichols, 2001.

p. 58: universities and industry, see Brown, 2000; Drum, 2001; Hall, et al., 2001; Birnbaum, 2002.

Chapter 3. Decline of Economic Diversity

p. 64: on large farms, see *Yes!,* 2000; K. Eriksson, 1999; Krome, 2001.

p. 67: recording industry, see Knox, 2000; *The Capital Times,* 2000a; Srinivasan, 2001.

p. 67: on digital watermarks and DMCA, see *IEEE Spectrum,* 2001; *Science,* 2001; Seebach, 2001; Cherry, 2001; Cherry and Siang, 2001.

p. 68: access issues for publications including electronic media, see Klein, 1999; Stallman, 2000; Jenkins, 2000; *Science,* 2000; Shulman, 2001.

p. 68: cultural diversity, see Gell-Mann, 1994; Maybury-Lewis, 1992a; Rifkin, 2001.

p. 68: court decisions on television, see *The Capital Times,* 2002a; 2002b.

p. 68: impact of acquisitions on radio, see Wineke, 2000b; Albertoni, 2001; Kot, 2002a.
p. 69: impact of global corporations on publishing, see Paz, 1991; Malakoff, 2000; Brodsky, et al., 2001.
p. 69: quality programs and control of suppliers, see Uzumeri, 1998.
p. 70: importance of interfaces, see Eriksson, 1995.
p. 71: movement to the margins of life by creative people, see Zachary, 2000.
p. 71: on diversity with area, see Mansur, 2000; Rosenzweig, 1999.
p. 71: grizzly bears and required habitat, see Chadwick, 2001.
p. 72: impact of loss of economic space, see Paz, 1991b.
p. 72: decline of diversity in books, see Paz, 1991c.
p. 73: physical and virtual mega-stores, see Smith, 2000.
p. 73: decline of diversity on Web, see Chester, 2001.
p. 73: Internet patents, see Hansell, 1999; Shulman, 2000.
p. 74: Linux operating system, see Comerford, 1999; Lucky, 1999; Korten, 1999c.
p. 74: on Internet service, see Garfinkel, 2002.
p. 77: star lecturers, see Noam, 1995.
p. 77: disk jockeys, see Albertoni, 2001.
p. 78: problems for free agents such as consultants, see Walker, 2001.
p. 78: plant closings and downsizing, see Bluestone, et al., 1982b; Luttwak, 1993; Luttwak, 1999.
p. 79: antibodies as metaphor for small businesses; see Paz, 1991c.
p. 80: nontraditional work and the economy, see Henderson, 1981; Korten, 1999d, 1999e; Luttwak, 1999c.
p. 81: on the use of numbers, see Roddick, 2001; Nichols, 2002.
p. 82: economic niches and the Internet, see *Harvard,* 1999.
p. 83: early paper on the use of the commons, see Hardin, 1968.
p. 83: shared use and management strategies, see Ostrom, et al., 1999.
p. 83: on loners and cooperative efforts, see Hauert, et al., 2002; *The Capital Times,* 2002c.

Chapter 4. Return to Adaptive Management

p. 87: scientific management and Taylor, see Zinn, 1980; Kanigel, 1997.
p. 88: quality control management systems, see Dobyns, et al., 1991; 1994; Hoerl, 1998; Curkovic, et al, 2000.
p. 89: systems theory, see Berlinski, 1976; Stacey, 1996; Eriksson, 1999.

p. 89: management of knowledge workers, see Drucker, 1973; 1989.
p. 89: engineering assumptions for analysis, see Walter, 2001.
p. 90: nonlinear behavior, see Stacey, 1996; Eriksson, 1998b, 1999b.
p. 90: emergent properties, see Anderson, 1972; Schweber, 1993.
p. 90: chaos, see Gleick, 1987; Waldrop, 1992.
p. 92: adaptive systems, see Widrow, et al., 1985.
p. 92: neural networks, see Haykin, 1994.
p. 92: self-organizing systems, see Lewin, 1992; Waldrop, 1992; Casti, 1994.
p. 93: adaptive management, see Eriksson, 1998; 1999; 2000.
p. 96: corporate management style, see Galbraith, 1992a.
p. 98: organizational memory, see Cross, et al., 2000.
p. 99: on link between speed and memory, see Kundera, 1997.
p. 101: aircraft carriers and flexible management, see Pool, 1997.
p. 101: on dangers of conformity, see Greising, 2002c.
p. 102: questions with TQM, see Rumbaugh, 2000; Trudel, 2000; Cross, et al., 2000; Trudel, 2001.
p. 103: flexible approaches in product engineering, see Kraemer, 2001.
p. 103: books on adaptive approaches to management, see Fradette and Michaud, 1998; Haeckel, 1999; Highsmith, 2000.
p. 103: articles on decentralized control, see Ungson and Trudel, 1999; Schonberger, 2000; Sawhney and Prandelli, 2001.

Chapter 5. Quest for Justice

p. 108: issues with growth, see Meadows, et al., 1972; Ross-Macdonald, 1977; *Woodlands,* 1977; Freeman, et al., 1978; *Woodlands,* 1979.
p. 108: ethics and justice, see *LCA,* 1980; *UW-Extension,* 1981; *LCA,* 1982; *WCC,* 1983.
p. 109: gap between rich and poor, see Korten, 1999f; Luttwak, 1999d; Crutsinger, 2000a; Milfred, 2000a.
p. 109: on co-opting agenda of protesters, see Longworth, 2002.
p. 109: on anti-globalization protests at in Davos, see Pfaff, 2001.
p. 110: viewing the market as God, see Cox, 1999; Frank, 2000.
p. 111: on the lack of direction or purpose in the market, see Paz, 1991d.
p. 111: rating student writing, see Baker, 2001.
p. 111: numbers in church, see Sevig, 2001.
p. 112: winners, see Frank and Cook, 1995.
p. 112: game shows, see Rogers, 2000.

p. 114: on mergers and culture, see Armour, 2000; Lohr, 2001.

p. 114: background on California power crisis, see Ilic, et al., 2001; Vogel, 2000; Holson, et al., 2001.

p. 114: discussions of pricing of electric power, see Vogel, 2000; Holson, et al., 2001; Berry, et al., 2001; Makansi, 2001; Overbye, et al., 2001.

p. 115: comments on capacity, see Vogel, et al., 2001.

p. 115: Telstar satellite, see Zimmerman, 2000; Eriksson, 2001.

p. 115: on vaccines and markets, see Reno, 2001b; *The Capital Times,* 2001; Cohen, 2002a; Cohen, et al., 2002b.

p. 116: on accounting issues related to Enron, see McRoberts, 2002; Ivins, 2002; Singhania, 2002.

p. 116: on role of regulatory and legal forces, see Narker, 2002.

p. 118: on stock prices and consumer spending; see Goozner, 2000.

p. 118: slow growth of factory wages, see Newman, 2000a; Anderson, 2000.

p. 118: on median wages, see *COWS,* 2000a; Hall, 2000; Eriksson, 2002.

p. 119: interest rates, see Crutsinger, 2000b; Goozner, 2000.

p. 119: issues on farm economy, see Galbraith, 1994b.

p. 120: on farm subsidies, see Brasher, 2000; Burns, 2002a; 2002b; 2002c.

p. 120: farms and factories, see Batra, 1993.

p. 120: working hours and quality of life, see Barrett, 2000c; Uchitelle, 2000; Lucht, 2000; Fraser, 2000; Wineke, 2001b; Lewin, 2000.

p. 120: on family income, see *COWS,* 2000b; Eriksson, 2002.

p. 121: on 1965 tax rates, see Samuelson, 1964.

p. 121: on 1980s tax cuts and income disparities, see Blinder, 1990.

p. 122: on tax cuts, see Ivins, 2001a; 2001b; J. Rogers, 2001; Wayne, 2001.

p. 122: 2001 tax cuts and gap between rich and poor, see Reno, 2001a.

p. 122: on state and local taxes in Wisconsin, see *COWS,* 2000b.

p. 123: on fees for library services, see Weier, 2002.

p. 123: tuition proposal, see Nathans, 2001.

p. 123: tuition and low income students, see Toppo, 2001.

p. 125: wage increases and work ethic, see Galbraith, 1992c.

p. 125: income and wealth distribution, see Luttwak, 1999c; Blinder, 1990.

p. 126: on general accounting concerns, see *Merrill Lynch,* 1999; Krantz, et al., 2001; Hunt, 2001; DeCarlo, et al., 2002.

p. 126: tax issues, see Johnston, 2000.

p. 126: on accounting issues related to Enron, see McRoberts, 2002; Ivins, 2002; Singhania, 2002.

p. 126: dominance of business language and values, see Hammer, 1996a.

p. 127: agri-culture vs. agriculture, see K. Eriksson, 2000.

p. 127: customers vs. students, see Brown, 2000.

p. 128: market paradigm in schools, see Lindgren, 1999.

p. 128: on shopping centers and consumerism, see Melnick, 2001.

p. 130: on prisons, see Balousek, 2000a; Luttwak, 1999b; Nathans, 2001; Dinur, 2002.

p. 131: on prison and farm statistics, see *Wisconsin Blue Book,* 2001-2002.

p. 132: on corporate buildings, see Rykwert, 2000; Wineke, 2001c.

p. 132: for a local example of naming rights and the issues that it raises, see Balousek, 2000b; Lueders, 2000; Wineke, 2000a.

p. 132: growth of large churches, see Bakopoulos, 2000.

p. 133: for a discussion of Pentecostal churches that have some of the same traits as this Lutheran church, see Cox, 1995.

p. 133: expanding nature of market, see Cox, 1999.

Chapter 6. Toward the Future

p. 136: books on global capitalism, see Luttwak, 1993; 1999 (review: Stern, 1999); Korten, 1995; 1997; 1999; Reich, 2000 (reviews: Franklin, 2001; Truly, 2001); Frank, 2000; Kelly, 2001.

p. 143: water utility and Internet access, see Balousek, 2002.

p. 145: on use of zoning to control developments, see Ivey, 2002d.

p. 145: on rejection of discount store proposal, see Ivey, 2002c.

p. 146: control of ownership, see K. Eriksson, 1999, p. 361; Newman, 2000d; Jones, 2002.

p. 148: on vaccines, see Cohen, 2002; Cohen, et al., 2002b.

p. 149: impact of closing of cheese factory, see Barrett, 2000a.

p. 150: small milk processing plants and producers, see K. Eriksson, 1999.

p. 150: proposals to assist local communities, see Bluestone, et al., 1982c.

p. 151: on local reviews of store proposals, see Ivey, 2002c.

p. 151: relationship of society and economy, see Luttwak, 1999b.

p. 152: on advisory councils, see Kenny, 2000.

p. 152: board opposition to shareholder proposal, see *DuPont,* 2000.

p. 153: local effects of plant closings, see Lucht, 2000.

p. 154: on corporations as persons, see Korten, 1999g; Kelly, 2001.

p. 156: on corporate responsibility and Enron collapse, see Murphy, 2002.

p. 156: on economy and personal relationships, see Maybury-Lewis, 1992b,c.

p. 158: for a discussion of Enron, see Simpson and McRoberts, 2002.

p. 159: on the treatment of corporations and accountants, see Greising, 2002b.

p. 160: on broader, less specific accounting rules, see Barnhart, 2002.

p. 160: NAFTA and FTAA, see Seligman, 2001; Sierra Club, 2000; *Public Citizen,* 2000; *Global Exchange,* 2000; Longworth, 2001; Nichols, 2001; Moyers, 2002.

p. 162: on comparative advantage, see Samuelson, 1964; Luttwak, 1993a.

p. 163: on economy in Argentina, see Smith, 2001; Rohter, 2002.

p. 165: on foreign aid expenditures, see *The Economist,* 2001.

p. 165: on direct aid to low income individuals, see Dunn, 2002.

p. 166: on legal actions by ABA and small bookstores, see Kravets, 2001.

p. 166: broadcasting industry, see Albertoni, 2001; Kot, 2002a, 2002b.

p. 167: on results of 2000 presidential election and policies of the new administration, see Moore, 2001.

p. 168: on fair trade conference, see Madison Fair Trade Action Alliance, 2002.

p. 168: on Sri Lanka milk prices, see ALRC, 2002; AHRC, 2001.

p. 169: on Wisconsin dairy prices, see Cropp, 1999.

p. 169: on new farm bill and subsidies, see Abbott, 2002; Cornwall, 2002; Burns, 2002a; 2002b; 2002c.

p. 172: on decisions to leave corporate world, see Carpenter, 2002.

p. 173: use of passive voice in government report, see Gavaghan, 2001.

p. 174: on decline in scientific tinkering, see Musser, 2002.

p. 176: on fair traded coffee and other products, see Darlington, 2002; Kalk, 2002; *Global Exchange,* 2001; *Equal Exchange,* 2000.

p. 179: emptying out, see Fox, 1988; Rupp, 1997; Wineke, 1999.

p. 180: on connections, see Palmer, 1998.

℘ *Bibliography* ℘

Abbott, Charles, "Senate passes farm bill boosting subsidies," *Reuters,* May 8, 2002 (www.reuters.com).

Adams, Henry, *The Education of Henry Adams,* Houghton Mifflin, Boston, 1961(originally published in 1918 by The Massachusetts Historical Society; see pp. 344-345 on concentrations of power).

Albertoni, Rich, "The rise of the chains" and "The decline of the DJ," *Isthmus,* October 5, 2001, pp. 14-18 (on the impact of deregulation on local radio and the declining role of the disk jockey).

Allman, William F., "Good news about noise," *U. S. News and World Report,* September 9, 1991, pp. 59-60 (on active sound control).

Alper, Joe, "Antinoise Creates the Sound of Silence," *Science,* April 26, 1991, pp. 508-509 (discusses active sound control and Digisonix).

Anderson, Curt, "House votes minimum wage up $1," *Wisconsin State Journal,* March 10, 2000 (includes plot of slow rise in minimum wage).

Anderson, P. W., "More is Different," *Science,* **177,** Aug. 4, 1972, 393-396 (early discussion of emergent properties in systems).

Armour, Stephanie, "Some experts foresee a clash of cultures," *USA Today,* January 11, 2000 (article relating to the proposed merger of America OnLine and Time Warner).

Baker, Gail Konop, "Writing taught wrongly," *Isthmus,* p. 10, March 2, 2001 (on attempts to quantify evaluations of student writing).

Bakopoulos, Dean, "Mega churches," *Isthmus,* December 22, 2000.

Balousek, Marv, "Crime rise projected for county," *Wisconsin State Journal,* May 21, 2000a.

Balousek, Marv, "Alliant buys naming rights to Expo Center," *Wisconsin State Journal,* June 1, 2000b.

Balousek, Marv, "High-speed Internet on tap in Sun Prairie," *Wisconsin State Journal,* April 3, 2002.

Barnhart, Bill, "How about auditing for investor?" *Chicago Tribune,* April 28, 2002 (on accounting rules).

Barrett, Rick, "Monroe cheese plant to close," *Wisconsin State Journal,* April 20, 2000a.

Barrett, Rick, "GE Medical is buying Lunar," *Wisconsin State Journal,* June 3, 2000b.

Barrett, Rick, "Number of working poor rises in state," *Wisconsin State Journal,* August 2, 2000c.

Batra, Ravi, *The Myth of Free Trade,* Simon and Schuster, 1993 (see pp. 58-67 on "agrification").

Beaver, William, "Is the Stakeholder Model Dead?" *IEEE Engineering Management Review,* **27** (3), Fall, 1999, pp. 80-84 (reprinted from *Business Horizons,* **42** (2), March - April, 1999, 8-12).

Bellman, Geoffrey M., *The Consultant's Calling,* Jossey-Bass, San Francisco, 1990.

Berlinski, David, *On Systems Analysis: An Essay Concerning the Limitations of Some Mathematical Methods in the Social, Political, and Biological Sciences,* The MIT Press, Cambridge, Mass., 1976.

Berry, Steve, and Riccardi, Nicholas, "Generators acted to keep prices higher, studies show," *latimes.com (The Los Angeles Times),* January 14, 2001.

Birnbaum, Howard K., "A personal reflection on university research funding," *Physics Today,* March, 2002, pp. 49-53 (see p. 52 on problems with industrial research support).

Blinder, Alan S., *Growing Together,* Whittle Books, The Larger Agenda Series, Knoxville, Tennessee, 1990 (a - see p.11 on tax cuts during 1980s; b - see p. 16-18 on income distribution; c - see pp. 19-20 on growth of income and taxes of top 1% of families from 1977-1990).

Bluestone, Barry, and Harrison, Bennett, *The Deindustrialization of America,* Basic Books, New York, 1982 (a - see pp. 153-155, 160-164 on problems of absentee ownership; b - see pp. 80-81 on the effects of plant closings; c - see pp. 238-239 on plant closings and communities).

Brand, Stewart, *The Clock of the Long Now,* Basic Books, New York, 1999, pp. 28-31.

Brasher, Philip, "Group's study finds big farms get majority of farm subsidies," *Wisconsin State Journal,* April 26, 2000.

Brezonick, Mike, "Cummins to Acquire Nelson Industries," *Diesel Progress,* January, 1998, pp. 56-57.

Broad, William J., "New Technology Defeats Unwanted Noise," *The New York Times,* June 30, 1987.

Brodsky, Marc H., and McIlrath, Thomas J., "Defending freedom of speech: What have we accomplished?" *Physics Today,* June, 2001, p. 10 (on cost of journals and lawsuits).

Brown, James Robert, "Privatizing the university -- the new tragedy of the commons," *Science,* December 1, 2000.

Burns, Greg, "High yield: the federal subsidy," *Chicago Tribune,* April 21, 2002a (on federal farm subsidies).

Burns, Greg, "Dairy farmers join herd at subsidy trough," *Chicago Tribune,* May 19, 2002b.

Burns, Greg, "A fresh crop of subsidies," *Chicago Tribune,* May 26, 2002c (discusses loophole for large producers).

Carlton, Jim, *Apple,* HarperCollins, New York, 1997 (see especially pp. 62-81).

Carpenter, Dave, "Baby boomer burnout: Leaving rat race and high salaries behind," *Wisconsin State Journal,* March 18, 2002.

Casti, John L., *Complexification: Explaining a Paradoxical World Through the Science of Surprise,* Harper Collins, New York, 1994.

Causey, James E., "Cincinnati Bank to Buy Firstar," *Milwaukee Journal Sentinel,* July 1, 1998.

Chadwick, Douglas H., "Grizzlies," *National Geographic,* **200** (1), July, 2001, pp. 2-25.

Chandler, Susan, "Trying to dodge a merger bullet," *Chicago Tribune,* May 19, 2002 (on Lands' End merger with Sears).

Cherry, Steven M., "Is Hyperlinking to Decryption Software Illegal?" *IEEE Spectrum,* August, 2001, pp. 64-65.

Cherry, Steven, and Siang, Sanyin, "Digital Millennium Copyright Act Faces Court Test," *IEEE Spectrum,* October, 2001, pp. 26-30.

Chester, Jeffrey A., "Web behind walls," *Technology Review,* June 2001, p. 94.

Cohen, Jon, "U.S. vaccine supply falls seriously short," *Science,* March 15, 2002a, pp. 1998-2001.

Cohen, Jon, and Marshall, Eliot, "Should the government make vaccines?" *Technology Review,* May, 2002b.

Colás, Santiago, *Postmodernity in Latin America,* Duke University Press, Durham, p. 6, 1994 (on the loss of nature and historicity).

Comerford, Richard, "The Path to Open-Source Systems," *IEEE Spectrum,* May, 1999, pp. 24-31 (see pp. 30-31 on Linux software).

Cornwall, Rupert, "Bush stokes trade war by signing farm subsidies bill," *Independent News,* Independent Digital (UK) Ltd., May 10, 2002 (http://news.independent.co.uk/world/americas/).

Cox, Harvey, *Fire from Heaven,* Addison-Wesley, New York, 1995 (on Pentecostal spirituality and implications for religion).

Cox, Harvey, "The Market as God," *The Atlantic Monthly,* March, 1999, pp. 18-23 (on our obsession with market principles).

Crichton, Michael, *Timeline,* Alfred A. Knopf, New York, 1999, pp. 400-401, 436-437 (fictional speech on history and corporate power).

Cropp, Bob, "Milk marketing orders and dairy compacts: Why the Upper Midwest concern?" *Dairy Initiatives Newsletter,* **8** (2), Fall, 1999 (http://www.ansci.umn.edu/dairy/dinews/milkmktorders.htm).

Cross, Rob, and Baird, Lloyd, "Technology is not enough; improving performance by building organization memory," *IEEE Engineering Management Review,* **28** (4), Fourth Quarter 2000, pp. 8-16 (originally published in *Sloan Management Review,* Spring, 2000, pp. 69-78).

Crutsinger, Martin, "Boom aside, rich-poor gap widens," *The Capital Times,* January 19, 2000a (provides information on unequal distribution of net worth; see also Luttwak and Milfred references).

Crutsinger, Martin, "Fed's rate hike just the beginning, analysts say," *Wisconsin State Journal,* February 3, 2000b (includes history of rates).

Curkovic, Sime, Melnyk, Steven, A., Handfield, Robert B., and Calantone, Roger, "Investigating the linkage between Total Quality Management and Environmentally Responsible Manufacturing," *IEEE Transactions On Engineering Management,* **47** (4), November, 2000, pp. 444-464.

Darlington, Tenaya, "Fertile ground for fair trade: Madisonians put their money where their politics are," *thedailypage.com,* Madison, March 8, 2002.

DeCarlo, Scott, and Maiello, Michael, "Faux forma," *Forbes,* April 15, 2002, p. 166 (on the use of pro forma results).

Dickey, Josh L., "CEO brothers seal $19 billion bank deal," *Wisconsin State Journal,* October 5, 2000 (on Firstar purchase of U.S. Bancorp).

Dinur, Esty, "Jailhouse spoiler," *Isthmus,* June 7, 2002 (on problems with Wisconsin's approach to corrections).

Ditlea, Steve, "The Real E-books," *Technology Review,* July/August, 2000, pp. 71-78 (see also Feedback letters, "All About E-books," *Technology Review,* Sept./Oct., 2000, p.17).

Dobyns, Lloyd, and Crawford-Mason, Clare, *Quality or Else: The Revolution in World Business,* Houghton Mifflen, New York, 1991.

Dobyns, Lloyd, and Crawford-Mason, Clare, *Thinking About Quality: Progress, Wisdom, and the Deming Philosophy,* Random House, New York, 1994.

Drucker, Peter, *Management: Tasks, Responsibilities, Practices,* Harper and Row, New York, 1973 (see chapter 52, pp. 627-636, on issues concerning corporate boards).

Drucker, Peter, *The New Realities,* Harper and Row, New York, 1989 (see pp. 227-228 on the legitimacy of management).

Drum, Ryan, "For-profit motives compromise academic mission, integrity," *Wisconsin State Journal,* January 7, 2001.

Dunn, Bill, "Academics ponder radical ways to close income gap," *The Capital Times,* April 30, 2002 (on direct aid to low income individuals).

Elmer-Dewitt, Philip, "Fighting noise with noise," *Time,* December 4, 1989, p. 94.

Erickson, Doug, "Wal-Mart in Ft. Atkinson no shoo-in," *Wisconsin State Journal,* January 7, 2001.

Eriksson, Karen R., *Adult Education and Social Change: Lessons from Rural Task Groups,* Ph.D. Dissertation, University of Wisconsin-Madison, 1999 (includes discussion of the "underground").

Eriksson, Karen R., private communication, May 4, 2000 (on the irony and implications of the use of "agri-business" versus the more inclusive and traditional "agri-culture/agriculture").

Eriksson, Larry J., *Active Sound Attenuation Using Adaptive Digital Signal Processing,* Ph.D. Thesis, UW-Madison, 1985.

Eriksson, L. J., "Active Sound Control," Chapter 15 in *Noise and Vibration Control Engineering,* edited by Leo L. Beranek and Istvan L. Ver, Wiley, New York, 1992 (review of the technology).

Eriksson, L. J., Allie, M. C., and Greiner, R. A., "A Case Study in University-Industry Cooperation on Active Sound and Vibration Control Research," *J. Acoust. Soc. Am.,* **95** (5), part 2, p. 2988 (abstract only), 1994, (the story of the formation of Digisonix).

Eriksson, L. J., "Living at the Interface," unpublished manuscript, May, 1995 (on the role of interfaces in innovation and change).

Eriksson, L. J., "Active Sound and Vibration Control: A Technology in Transition," *Noise Control Eng. J.,* **44** (1), Jan.-Feb., 1996, pp. 1-9.

Eriksson, Larry J., "The Impact of Adaptive Approaches on Management and Technology," Eriksson Research, Madison, 1998, 1999 (also *Adaptive Management: Growing Beyond Management by Control,* presentation to MABC, Madison, November 14, 2000).

Eriksson, L. J., "Politics vs. Engineering," *American Heritage of Invention and Technology,* **16** (3), Winter, 2001, p. 5 (letter) (comments on government and *Telstar;* see also Zimmerman, 2000).

Eriksson, L. J., "Economic inequities and corporate accountability," *Corporate Accountability Packet,* Wisconsin Network for Peace and Justice, Madison, Wisconsin, February, 2002, pp. 9-11.

Farnham, Alan, "Migratory Habits of the 500," *Fortune,* April 24, 1989, pp. 400-401 (on losses of corporate headquarters from 1978-88).

Fitzgerald, Sean, "Wal-Mart announces Supercenter," *The Door County Advocate,* July 28, 2000a.

Fitzgerald, Sean, "What will happen to Wal-Mart store?" *The Door County Advocate,* August 1, 2000b.

Fox, Matthew, *The Coming of the Cosmic Christ,* Harper and Row, San Francisco, 1988 (see p. 162 on need for emptying as part of rebirth).

Fradette, Michael, and Michaud, Steve, *The Power of Corporate Kinetics: Create the Self-Adapting, Self-Renewing, Instant-Action Enterprize,* Simon and Schuster, New York, 1998.

Frank, Robert H., and Cook, Philip J., *The Winner-Take-All Society,* Free Press, New York, 1995.

Frank, Thomas, *One Market Under God,* Anchor Books, New York, 2000.

Franklin, Stephen, "The too-fast track," *Chicago Tribune,* January 28, 2001 (a book review of *The Future of Success* by Robert Reich).

Fraser, Jill Andresky, *White Collar Sweatshop: The Deterioration of Work and Its Rewards in Corporate America,* W. W. Norton, New York, 2000.

Freeman, Christopher, and Jahoda, Marie, eds., *World Futures: The Great Debate,* Universe Books, New York, 1978.

Gaines, Sallie L., "Scholars' clearinghouse," *Wisconsin State Journal,* September, 12, 1999 (on consulting group of academic scholars).

Galbraith, John Kenneth, *The Culture of Contentment,* Houghton Mifflin, New York, 1992 (a - see pp. 68-69 on delegation of thought and problems; b - see pp. 53-56 on management power; c - see pp. 13-15 on the affluent and the poor).

Galbraith, John Kenneth, *A Journey Through Economic Time,* Houghton Mifflin, New York, 1994, (a - see p. 203 on relationship between shareholders, management, and directors; b - see pp. 59-60, 75-77, and 200 on the special treatment of agriculture).

Garfinkel, Simson, "The Internet Amenity," *Technology Review,* March, 2002, pp. 33-34 (on provision of free wireless Internet access).

Gavaghan, Helen, "Mission to Saturn Rises from Ashes," *Science,* **293,** July 13, 2001, p. 193 (on error "caused by the system").

Gell-Mann, Murray, *The Quark and the Jaguar,* W. H. Freeman, New York, 1994 (see p. 338 on the preservation of cultural diversity).

Gleick, James, *Chaos,* Viking, New York, 1987.

Goozner, Merrill, "Economy races toward rate hike," *Chicago Tribune,* January 29, 2000 (stock prices and consumer spending; debate over wage increases).

Greene, Bob, "Who do you really think you work for?" *Chicago Tribune*, April 2, 2001 (on externalizing of costs through use of automated telephone service).

Greising, David, "HP board fracas a worthy model for directors," *Chicago Tribune*, March 6, 2002a (on proposed merger with Compaq).

Greising, David, "Is Anderson furor letting Enron off hook?" *Chicago Tribune*, March 31, 2002b.

Greising, David, " 'Boot camp' failed to teach all they could be," *Chicago Tribune*, April 21, 2002c (on shortcomings of conformity and standardization).

Gribble, Roger A., "Sold: Mattel Could Spur Growth of Pleasant Co.," *Wisconsin State Journal*, June 16, 1998.

Haeckel, Stephan H., *Adaptive Enterprise: Creating and Leading Sense-and-Respond Organizations*, Harvard Business School Press, Boston, 1999.

Hall, Dee J., "Report: workers fare well in state," *The Wisconsin State Journal*, September 4, 2000 (despite headline, this article summarizes *COWS* report on decline in Wisconsin wages from 1979-1999).

Hall, Zach W., and Scott, Christopher, "University-industry partnership," editorial, *Science*, **291**, January 26, 2001, p. 553.

Hammer, Michael, *Beyond Reengineering*, Harper Business, New York, 1996 (a - pp. xiv-xv for comments on the dominance of business language in our lives; b - pp. 67-68 on burnout in corporate world).

Hansell, Saul, "Patents reshaping online shopping," *Wisconsin State Journal*, December 25, 1999.

Hardin, Garrett, "The Tragedy of the Commons," *Science*, **162**, p. 1243, 1968.

Harkavy, Jerry, "Striking a New Balance: Athletic footwear maker works to stay domestic," *The Capital Times*, March 2-3, 2002.

Hauert, Christoph; De Monte, Silvia; Hofbauer, Josef; and Sigmund, Karl, "Volunteering as Red Queen mechanism for cooperation in public goods games," *Science*, **296**, pp. 1129-1132, 2002 (see also *This Week in Science*, Phil Szuromi, ed., pp. 977, 979).

Haykin, Simon, *Neural Networks*, Macmillan, New York, 1994.

Henderson, Hazel, *The Politics of the Solar Age,* Anchor Books, Garden City, New York, 1981.

Highsmith, James A. III, *Adaptive Software Development,* Dorset House, New York, 2000.

Hoerl, Roger W., "Six Sigma and the Future of the Quality Profession," *IEEE Engineering Management Review,* **26** (3), Fall, 1998, pp. 87-94 (reprinted from American Society for Quality, 1997).

Holson, Laura M., and Oppel, Jr., Richard A., "Trying to follow the money in California's energy mess," *The New York Times on the Web,* January 12, 2001.

Hunt, Jr., Isaac C., "Accountants as Gatekeepers -- Adding Security and Value to the Financial Reporting System," speech to Federation of Schools of Accountancy, Arlington, Virginia, October 26, 2001 (available on Oct. 31, 2001, at www.sec.gov/news/speech/spch518.htm).

Ilic, Marija, Skantze, Petter, and Visudhiphan, Poonsaeng, "Electricity troubles in California: who's next?" *IEEE Spectrum,* February, 2001, pp. 11-13.

Ivey, Mike, "When firms are sold off, nothing is for certain," *The Capital Times,* December 6-7, 1997a (on the sale of Nelson).

Ivey, Mike, " 'Time right' for sale of Nelson Industries," *The Capital Times,* December 5, 1997b.

Ivey, Mike, "Firstar, U.S. Bancorp to merge," *The Capital Times,* October 4, 2000.

Ivey, Mike, "Big national paint maker buys Mautz," *The Capital Times,* November 8, 2001.

Ivey, Mike, "Old paint," *The Capital Times,* April 9, 2002a (on closing of Mautz paint plant in Madison).

Ivey, Mike, "Companies show it pays to play by the rules," *Capital Times,* April 23, 2002b (rankings by *Business Ethics*; see www.businessethics.com).

Ivey, Mike, "East side Sam's Club rejected," *Capital Times,* May 21, 2002c.

Ivey, Mike, "The economic argument against big box," *Capital Times,* June 11, 2002d (on economic impact statements and zoning laws).

Ivins, Molly, "It stinks!" *The Capital Times,* February 19, 2001a (on Bush tax cut proposal).

Ivins, Molly, "Stimulus package lets the rich annex the treasury," *The Capital Times,* November 5, 2001b (on tax cuts for the wealthy).

Ivins, Molly, "Enron's 'aggressive accounting' is just part of rot," *The Capital Times,* January 30, 2002 (on of the collapse of Enron).

Jenkins, Henry, "Digital land grab," *Technology Review,* March/April, 2000, pp. 103-105 (discusses ownership of fictional characters).

Jones, Patrice M., "Brazil's Globo television network girds for global economy," *Chicago Tribune,* May 28, 2002 (on foreign investors).

Johnston, David Jay, "Corporations growing bolder with tax dodges," *Wisconsin State Journal,* February, 27, 2000.

Kalk, Samara, "Coffee with a purpose: Fair trade office opens," *The Capital Times,* March 15, 2002 (on *Equal Exchange* office).

Kanigel, Robert, *The One Best Way,* Viking, New York, 1997 (on Frederick Winslow Taylor and scientific management).

Kelly, Marjorie, *The Divine Right of Capital,* Berrett-Koehler, San Francisco, 2001 (see pp. 159-172 on corporations and personhood).

Kenny, Roger M., "Rediscovering advisory boards," *IEEE Engineering Management Review,* **28** (4), Fourth Quarter, 2000, pp. 24-27 (originally published in *Directors & Boards*).

Klein, Joshua, "Sony's Century," *The Onion A. V. Club,* **35** (47), December 23, 1999 - January 19, 2000 (access to older recordings).

Knaapen, Joe, "Comments on Target are Mixed," *The Door County Advocate,* March 10, 2000a.

Knaapen, Joe, "Target clears first city hurdle," *The Door County Advocate,* May 26, 2000b.

Knaapen, Joe, "A tale of two discount stores," *The Door County Advocate,* August 11, 2000c.

Knox, Noelle, "Time Warner, EMI planning merger," *Wisconsin State Journal,* January 24, 2000 (subsequently dropped).

Korten, David C., *When Corporations Rule The World,* Berrett-Koehler Publishers, San Francisco, California, 1995.

Korten, David C., "Money vs. Wealth," *YES! A Journal of Positive Futures,* Spring, 1997 (http://www.futurenet.org/2money) (discusses externalization of corporate costs and concentrated power and wealth).

Korten, David C., *The Post-Corporate World: Life After Capitalism,* Berrett-Koehler Publishers, San Francisco, California, and Kumarian Press, West Hartford, Connecticut, 1999 (a - see pp. 164-167 on discount stores; b - see pp. 46-48 and p. 194 on corporate cost externalization; c - see p. 175 on Linux; d - see p. 75-76 on expectations for corporate managers; e - see p. 70 on the distortions in accounting; f - see pp. 79-83 on the growing inequality of the distribution of wealth; g - see pp. 183-186 on corporations as persons).

Kot, Greg, "Rocking radio's world," *Chicago Tribune,* April 14, 2002a (on problems associated with consolidations in the radio industry).

Kot, Greg, "Music industry raises its voice for radio reforms," *Chicago Tribune,* May 23, 2002b.

Kraemer, Thomas, "Printing enters the jet age," *American Heritage of Invention and Technology,* **17** (4), Spring, 2001, pp. 18-27 (on the value of an adaptive approach to product development).

Krantz, Matt, and Farrell, Greg, "Fuzzy accounting raises flags," *USA Today,* June 22, 2001, p. 1B.

Kravets, David, "Booksellers antitrust suit fizzles," *The Capital Times,* April 20, 2001.

Krome, Margaret, "Inefficiencies of scale," *The Capital Times,* January 25, 2001 (problems with large scale farms).

Kundera, Milan, *Slowness,* HarperPerennial, New York, 1997, p. 39.

Kuo, Sen M., and Morgan, Dennis R., *Active Noise Control Systems,* Wiley-Interscience, New York, 1996 (a review of the technology).

Levering, Robert, and Moskowitz, Milton, *The 100 Best Companies to Work for in America,* Plume/Dutton Signet, New York, Revised Edition, 1993, pp. 83-88 (includes Cummins).

Lewin, Roger, *Complexity: Life at the Edge of Chaos,* Macmillan, New York, 1992.

Lewin, Tamar, "Two-income families now the norm," *Wisconsin State Journal,* Oct. 24, 2000.

Lindgren, Amy, "To succeed, U.S. workers must embrace knowledge age, author says," *Wisconsin State Journal,* March 14, 1999 (example of the use of terms such as "markets" and "customers" in education and religion).

Lohr, Steve, "Clash over legacy fuels computer merger battle," *The New York Times,* November 18, 2001 (on proposed merger of HP and Compaq).

Longworth, R. C., "Laws skirted using NAFTA," *Chicago Tribune,* July 5, 2001 (on Chapter 11 of NAFTA regarding environmental and labor rules).

Longworth, R. C., "After the mainstream has stolen your agenda," *Chicago Tribune,* February 10, 2002 (on co-opting protest movement).

Lucht, Beth, "Out in the cold," *Isthmus,* December 8, 2000 (on plant closing).

Lucky, Robert W., "Free Software," *IEEE Spectrum,* May, 1999, p. 24 (discussion of Linux).

Lueders, Bill, "What the Alliant deal does," *Isthmus,* June 23, 2000.

Luttwak, Edward, *The Endangered American Dream,* Simon and Schuster, New York, 1993 (a - see p. 147 on importance of location of home office; b - see pp. 23-27 on issues with comparative advantage).

Luttwak, Edward, *Turbo Capitalism: Winners and Losers in the Global Economy,* Harper Collins, New York, 1999 (a - see pp. 236-237 on society serving the economy; b - see pp. 1-26 on winners and losers; c - see pp. 212-213 on impact of elder care costs on the GNP; d - see pp. 85-101 and Crutsinger (2000a) on inequality of wealth distribution, also Milfred (2000a) on income).

Makansi, Jason, "California's electricity crisis rooted in many failings," *IEEE Spectrum,* February, 2001, pp. 24-28.

Malakoff, David, "Librarians seek to block merger of scientific publishing giants," *Science,* November 3, 2000, pp. 910-911.

Maloney, Lawrence D., "Air Travel Enters the Quiet Zone," *Design News,* September, 12, 1994, pp.78,80,82 (contains discussion of Lord Corporation and Digisonix).

Mansur, Michael, "Study shows benefits of biodiversity," *Wisconsin State Journal,* May 30, 2000.

Maybury-Lewis, David, *Millennium: Tribal Wisdom and the Modern World,* Viking, New York, 1992 (a - see p. 267-8 and 278-280 on Cultural Survival; b - see p. 68 on people, economics, and modern society; c - see p. 87 on people and values).

McRoberts, Flynn, "The Enron effect shakes nation's investor culture," *Chicago Tribune,* January 27, 2002.

Meadows, Donnella H., Meadows, Dennis L., Randers, Jorgen, and Behrens, III, William W., *The Limits to Growth,* Universe Books, New York, 1972.

Melnick, Andrew J., "Terrorism vs. Consumerism," *Global Research Highlights,* Merrill Lynch, November 16, 2001 (consumerism as secular faith).

Milam, Stan, "Limited term workers take full-time spots," *Wisconsin State Journal,* Oct. 1, 2000.

Milfred, Scott, "Rich make 8 times as much as the poor," *Wisconsin State Journal,* January 18, 2000a (on inequality in income).

Milfred, Scott, "State 41st in personal wealth," *Wisconsin State Journal,* June 9, 2000b (comments on Wisconsin's lack of corporate headquarters).

Moore, Michael, *Stupid White Men,* ReganBooks imprint of HarperCollins, New York, 2001 (includes discussion of 2000 presidential election and actions of new Bush administration).

Moyers, Bill, "Trading democracy," *Bill Moyers Reports,* broadcast on Public Television, February 5, 2002 (on NAFTA).

Murphy, Caryle, "Clergy call Enron executives' behavior as they see it - sin," *Chicago Tribune,* March 5, 2002 (includes comments on responsibilities of corporations to the community).

Musser, George, "R.I.P. for D.I.Y.," *Scientific American,* May, 2002, p. 26 (on the decline in scientific tinkering and do-it-yourself projects).

Nairn, Geoff, "Sound of silence," *Financial Times,* December 6, 1994 (the use of active sound control on aircraft and Digisonix).

Narker, Steven R., "Letting the sun shine in," *Global Research Highlights,* Merrill Lynch, February 1, 2002 (on regulations and the legal system in the self-correcting nature of American capitalism).

Nathans, Aaron, "New budget socks UW, its students," *The Capital Times,* February 21, 2001.

Newman, Judy, "Nelson Industries sale looks to future," *Wisconsin State Journal,* Dec. 5, 1997a.

Newman, Judy, "Acquisition called a good fit," *Wisconsin State Journal,* December 5, 1997b (discusses Nelson merger with Cummins).

Newman, Judy, "Factory work is back, but at wages that aren't nearly as attractive as before," *Wisconsin State Journal,* February 27, 2000a.

Newman, Judy, "Rowley-Schlimgen is acquired," *Wisconsin State Journal,* August, 15, 2000b.

Newman, Judy, "No big changes for Firstar," *Wisconsin State Journal,* October 5, 2000c.

Newman, Judy, "Alliant suit cites rules," *Wisconsin State Journal,* October 21, 2000d.

Nichols, John, "Fast track power no test of patriotism," *The Capital Times,* October 9, 2001 (on issues related to FTAA).

Nichols, John, "Globalization's evils laid out," *The Capital Times,* January 25, 2002 (review of *Take It Personally: How Globalization Affects You and Powerful Ways to Challenge It* by Anita Roddick).

Nin, Anais, *The Voice,* a novelette published in *Winter of Artifice,* The Swallow Press, Chicago, 1948 (p. 120).

Noam, Eli M., "Electronics and the Dim Future of the University," *Science,* October 13, 1995, pp. 247-249.

Ostrom, Elinor; Burger, Joanna; Field, Christopher B.; Norgaard, Richard B.; Policansky, David; "Revisiting the Commons: Local Lessons, Global Challenges," *Science,* April 9, 1999, pp. 278-282 (on sharing of resources).

Overbye, Thomas J. and Weber, James D., "Visualizing the electric grid," *IEEE Spectrum,* February, 2001, pp. 52-58.

Palmer, Parker, *The Courage to Teach,* Jossey-Bass Publishers, San Francisco, California, 1998 (see pp. 11-16 and 54-56 on connections).

Patton, Naomi, "Speaker: History cuts to the truth," *Wisconsin State Journal,* April 19, 2000 (about the work of Howard Zinn).

Paz, Octavio, *The Other Voice: Essays on Modern Poetry,* Harcourt, Brace, Jovanovich, New York, 1991 (a - see p. 126 on comparing poets to miners; b - see pp. 112-114 on large publishers and shrinkage of here and now; c - see pp. 125-128 on small publishers as antibodies; d - see pp. 144-147 on problems with the market).

Pfaff, William, " 'Other Davos' latest signal of resistance to U. S. global vision," *Chicago Tribune,* January 30, 2001 (on violent encounters between protesters and police at World Economic Forum).

Pool, Robert, "When Failure is not an Option," *Technology Review,* July, 1997 (Reprinted in the *IEEE Engineering Management Review,* **27** (1), Spring, 1999, 27-31; on the flexible operation of aircraft carriers).

Quinones, Eric R., "What Happens When Corporate Culture Clash?" *Wisconsin State Journal,* December 3, 1998 (article about Exxon and Mobil).

Reich, Robert B., *The Future of Success,* Knopf, New York, 2000.

Reno, Robert, "W's tax cut helps the super rich widen the wealth gap," *The Capital Times,* June 6, 2001a.

Reno, Robert, "Rethinking free markets," *The Capital Times,* Oct. 16, 2001b.

Richgels, Jeff, "Sears to buy Lands' End," *The Capital Times,* May 13, 2002.

Riddle, Jennifer, "Ford, Stoughton company deal on sound technology," *Wisconsin State Journal,* May 15, 1992.

Rifkin, Jeremy, "Give cultural activists a seat at global table," *The Capital Times,* July 9, 2001.

Roddick, Anita, *Take It Personally: How Globalization Affects You and Powerful Ways to Challenge It,* Conari Press, Berkeley, California, 2002.

Rogers, Joel, "Stimulus is anything but," *The Capital Times,* November 5, 2001 (on tax cuts for the wealthy).

Rogers, Nicole E., "Watching me watching you," *Wisconsin State Journal,* July 7, 2000.

Rohter, Larry, "South American nations endure uncertain times," *Chicago Tribune,* April 13, 2002 (on slow growth in the 1990s during privatization and deregulation compared to earlier periods when there was more governmental intervention in the economy).

Rosenzweig, Michael L., "Heeding the Warning in Biodiversity's Basic Law," *Science,* April 9, 1999, pp. 276-277 (on area and loss of biodiversity).

Ross-Macdonald, Malcolm, *Life in the Future,* Doubleday, New York, 1977.

Rumbaugh, Jr., Max E., "Are commitments to quality waning?" *SAE Automotive Engineering International,* p. 8 (Focus), July, 2000.

Rupp, Joyce, *The Cup of Our Life,* Ave Maria Press, 1997.

Rykwert, Joseph, *The Seduction of Place: The City in the Twenty-first Century,* Schocken Books, 2000 (on dominance of private and corporate buildings).

Samuelson, Paul A., *Economics: An Introductory Analysis,* McGraw-Hill, New York, 1964 (6th ed.) (see p. 660-683 on trade; see p. 168 for 1965 tax rates).

Savage, Mark, "Cummins to buy Stoughton firm," *Milwaukee Journal Sentinel,* December 5, 1997.

Sawhney, Mohanbir, and Prandelli, Emanuela, "Communities of creation: Managing distributed innovation in turbulent markets," *IEEE Engineering Management Review,* **29** (1), First Quarter, 2001, pp. 6-24 (discusses emergent self-organization).

Schonberger, Richard J., "Economy of control," *IEEE Engineering Management Review,* **28** (4), Fourth Quarter, 2000, pp. 28-34.

Schweber, Silvan S., "Physics, Community and the Crisis in Physical Theory," *Physics Today,* Nov., 1993, 34-40 (on emergent properties of systems).

Seebach, Linda, "Digital copyright law threatens civil liberties," *Rocky Mountain News,* August 25, 2001.

Seligman, Dan, "The Next NAFTA?" *Yes! A Journal of Positive Futures,* Spring, 2001, pp. 6-7 (on the effects of NAFTA and the proposed FTAA).

Bibliography

Seppa, Nathan, "Noise creates silence," *Wisconsin State Journal,* February 25, 1992 (on Digisonix work on active sound control).

Sevig, Julie, "Numbers game," *The Lutheran,* January, 2001.

Shaw, Mike, "Council approves Target light," *The Door County Advocate,* February 1, 2000.

Shulman, Seth, "Software patents tangle the Web," *Technology Review,* March/April, 2000, pp. 68-76.

Shulman, Seth, "Looting the library," *Technology Review,* June, 2001.

Silver, Jonathan D., "Their product could be music to your ears," *The Capital Times,* March 11, 1992a (article on active control).

Simpson, Cam, and McRoberts, Flynn, "Architects of success and scandel," *Chicago Tribune,* January 20, 2002 (on culture at Enron).

Singhania, Lisa, " 'Enron effect' jolts investors," *The Capital Times,* January 30, 2002.

Smith, Elliot Blair, "Argentina teeters on brink despite $8B more in aid," *USA Today,* August 23, 2001.

Smith, Susan Lampert, "Grocery war flares in towns; Independents try to figure a way to compete with a big national operation," *Wisconsin State Journal,* March 12, 2000.

Srinivasan, Kalpana, "A mega prenuptial agreement," *The Capital Times,* January 12, 2001 (regarding the America OnLine and Time Warner merger).

Stacey, Ralph, "Management and the Science of Complexity: If Organizational Life is Nonlinear, Can Business Strategies Prevail?" *Research-Technology Management,* May-June, 1996, 8-10.

Stallman, Richard, "Freedom -- or Copyright?" *Technology Review,* May/June, 2000, p. 32 (on cost and control of e-books).

Stern, Larry, "Winning and losing, big," *IEEE Spectrum,* December, p. 10, 1999 (a review of Edward Luttwak's book, *Turbo Capitalism*).

Tarrant, John J., *Drucker: The Man Who Invented The Corporate Society,* Cahners, Boston, 1976 (see pp. 54-55 and 138-139 on corporate legitimacy).

Teitelman, Robert, "Enron: The tale less trumpeted," *IEEE Spectrum,* March, 2002, pp. 25-28 (on changes in corporate governance).

Toppo, Greg, "Rising costs keep poor out of college," *The Capital Times,* February 21, 2001.

Trudel, John D., "Innovation in sight," *IEEE Engineering Management Review,* **28** (4), Fourth Quarter 2000, pp. 6-7 (discusses limitations of TQM).

Trudel, John D., "Innovation in sight," *IEEE Engineering Management Review,* **29** (3), Third Quarter 2001, pp. 6-7 (on limitations of control).

Truly, Pat, "Reich's take on the new economy," *Wisconsin State Journal,* March 4, 2001.

Uchitelle, Louis, "Working families strain to live middle-class life," *The New York Times,* September, 10, 2000.

Ungson, Gerardo R., and Trudel, John D., "The Emerging Knowledge-Based Economy," *IEEE Spectrum,* May, 1999, pp. 60-65 (on centralized control).

Updike, John, *Rabbit is Rich,* Alfred A. Knopf, Inc. New York, 1981.

Uzumeri, Mustafa V., "ISO 9000 and Other Metastandards: Principles for Management Practice?" *IEEE Engineering Management Review,* **26** (3), Fall, 1998, pp. 5-15 (reprinted from *Academy of Management Executive,* **11** (1)).

Vogel, Nancy, "How state's consumers lost with electricity deregulation," *latimes.com (The Los Angeles Times),* December 9, 2000.

Vogel, Nancy, and Riccardi, Nicholas, "Blackouts stem from broad mix of reasons," *latimes.com (The Los Angeles Times),* January 19, 2001.

Waldrop, M. Mitchell, *Complexity: The Emerging Science at the Edge of Order and Chaos,* Simon and Schuster, NY, 1992.

Walter, Patrick L., "40 years of measurement engineering short courses -- has the end arrived?" *Sound and Vibration,* **35** (2), pp. 4-5 (editorial) February, 2001 (on assumptions for engineering analysis).

Walker, Rob, "Personal Days," *The New York Times,* April 29, 2001 (book review of *Free Agent Nation* by Daniel H. Pinknotes; Walker's review discusses downside to free agent work for many people).

Wayne, Leslie, "So, friend, it's time for that tax cut," *The New York Times,* November 18, 2001.

Weier, Anita, "Free library use on chopping block," *The Capital Times,* March 18, 2002.

White, Michael, "Kraft chief goes to Mattel," *Wisconsin State Journal,* May 18, 2000 (includes comments on priority given to shareholders).

Widrow, Bernard, and Stearns, Samuel D., *Adaptive Signal Processing,* Prentice-Hall, Englewood Cliffs, N.J., 1985.

Williams, Rosalind, *Notes on the Underground,* The MIT Press, Cambridge, 1990 (underground as metaphor for technological society).

Wineke, William R., comments on *The Cup of Our Life* by Joyce Rupp, *Wisconsin State Journal,* March 21, 1999.

Wineke, Bill, "Naming buildings has a price," *Wisconsin State Journal,* October 7, 2000a.

Wineke, William R., "Limbaugh shifts to WIBA," *Wisconsin State Journal,* October 21, 2000b.

Wineke, William R., "Many nonprofit groups face a staffing crisis," *Wisconsin State Journal,* February 11, 2001a (on finding directors).

Wineke, William R., "A grim workplace portrait," *Wisconsin State Journal,* February 25, 2001b (book review of *White Collar Sweatshop: The Deterioration of Work and Its Rewards in Corporate America* by Jill Andresky Fraser).

Wineke, William R., "An author argues that we are losing our urban architecture and, with it, our soul," *Wisconsin State Journal,* March 25, 2001c (book review of *The Seduction of Place: The City in the Twenty-first Century* by Joseph Rykwert).

Zachary, G. Pascal, "Silicon Handcuffs," *Technology Review,* May/June, 2000, p. 36 (on movement of creative people to margins).

Zimmerman, Robert, "Telstar," *American Heritage of Invention and Technology,* **16** (2), Fall, 2000, pp. 10-17 (see also Eriksson, 2001).

Zinn, Howard, *A People's History of the United States,* Harper and Row, New York, 1980.

---, *Alternatives to Growth '77,* "The Nature of Growth in Equitable and Sustainable Societies," October 2-4, 1977, The Woodlands, Texas.

---, *Third Biennial Woodlands Conference on Growth Policy,* "The Management of Sustainable Growth," October 28-31, 1979, The Woodlands, Texas.

---, *Consultation on Ethics and Energy,* sponsored by the Wisconsin Upper Michigan Synod of the LCA at the St. Joseph's Retreat House, April 18-20, 1980, Stevens Point, Wisconsin.

---, *Power, Poverty, and Politics,* sponsored by UW-Extension and others, February 7, March 7, and May 2, 1981, Madison, Wisconsin.

---, *Act on the Word,* sponsored by the Wisconsin Upper Michigan Synod of the LCA at the American Baptist Assembly Grounds, March 19-21, 1982, Green Lake, Wisconsin.

---, *Economic Problems and Policy - The Emerging Environment for the Mission of Midwestern Churches,* sponsored by The Church in Society Commission of the WCC, October 14-15, 1983.

---, *The First Fifty Years: 1939-1989,* Nelson Industries, Inc., Stoughton, Wisconsin, 1989.

---, "Nelson Industries and Ford Dedicate Joint Development Center," Digisonix Press Release, Middleton, Wisconsin, February 3, 1992a.

---, "Nelson Industries Reorganizes and Expands Digisonix Division," Digisonix Press Release, Middleton, Wisconsin, February 21, 1992b.

---, "Digisonix license to Ford," *The Capital Times,* May 15, 1992.

---, "Digisonix deals with Lord Corp.," *Wisconsin State Journal,* April 14, 1994.

---, "Nelson Industries to Merge into Cummins Engine Co.," Nelson Press Release, Stoughton, Wisconsin, December 4, 1997.

---, "Cummins Engine to Acquire Nelson Industries," Cummins Press Release, Columbus, Indiana, December 4, 1997a.

---, *1997 Annual Report,* Cummins Engine Company, Inc., Columbus, Indiana, 1997b (includes Nelson).

---, "The Wired Society," *Harvard Magazine,* May-June, 1999, 42-53, 106-107 (panel discussion on the Internet).

---, "If only we could get the answer from earnings," *Theme & Profile Investing Overview,* Merrill Lynch, December, 1999.

---, "EMI, Time Warner to merge music units," *The Capital Times,* January 24, 2000a (subsequently dropped).

---, *Proxy Statement,* DuPont, Wilmington, Delaware, March 17, 2000 (on opposition to shareholder proposal concerning plant closings).

---, "Food for Life (issue theme)," *Yes! A Journal of Positive Futures,* Summer, 2000 (includes article on costs of corporate farming).

---, "Taking the Pledge," *Science,* November 3, 2000, p. 915 (on access to scientific articles).

---, "NFATA's seventh anniversary: 'Taking Away' our clean environment," The Sierra Club, www.sierraclub.org/trade/action.asp, December 22, 2000 (on NAFTA and proposed FTAA).

---, "Executive Summary - The State of Working Wisconsin: 2000," *Center on Wisconsin Strategy (COWS),* University of Wisconsin-Madison, Madison, Wisconsin, 2000a (Figure 8 uses data in *COWS* report from analysis of Current Population Survey (CPS) data).

---, "The State of Working Wisconsin: 2000," *Center on Wisconsin Strategy (COWS),* University of Wisconsin-Madison, Madison, Wisconsin, 2000b, pp. 20-22 (Figure 9 uses data in *COWS* report from *Pulling Apart* by the Economic Policy Institute and Center on Budget and Policy Priorities, 2000).

---, "Top Ten Reasons to Oppose the Free Trade Area of the Americas," *Global Exchange,* www.globalexchange.org.

---, "Unveiling 'NAFTA for the Americas,' " *Public Citizen/Global Trade Watch,* www.citizen.org/pctrade/FTAA/factsheet.htm.

---, "Annual Report 2000," *Equal Exchange,* www.equalexchange.com.

---, "Foreign aid," *The Economist,* March 3, 2001 (includes data on contributions of nations by percentage of Gross Domestic Product).

---, "Talking about digital copyright," *IEEE Spectrum,* Spectral Lines, June, 2001, p. 9.

---, "Cracking the code," *Science,* ScienceScope, June 15, 2001, p. 1983.

---, "Working Wisconsin: Update 2001," *Center on Wisconsin Strategy (COWS),* University of Wisconsin-Madison, Madison, Wisconsin, September 2, 2001 (on wages).

---, "Update Sri Lanka: Mothers' activity to reduce milk prices; companies and government's response," *Asian Human Rights Commission (AHRC),* Urgent Appeals Program, September 14, 2001 (http://www.ahrchk.net/ua/mainfile.php/2001/165/).

---, "U. S. suffers chronic shortage of vaccines," *The Capital Times,* October 19, 2001 (on failure of market).

---, "Fair trade coffee campaign," *Global Exchange,* San Francisco, California, 2001 (see www.globalexchange.org/economy/coffee).

---, *Wisconsin Blue Book, 2001-2002,* compiled by Wisconsin Legislative Reference Bureau, Joint Committee on Legislative Organization, Wisconsin Legislature, Madison (see p. 612 on farms; see p. 813 on prisons).

---, "Court deals blow to TV ownership limits," *The Capital Times,* February 20, 2002a (rejects ownership rules on TV stations and cable).

---, "Milk Prices in Sri Lanka," *Asian Legal Resource Centre (ALRC),* March 4, 2002 (http://www.alrc.net/mainfile.php/58written/57/).

---, "FCC told to revisit rules," *The Capital Times,* April 3, 2002b (rejects rules concerning ownership of television stations).

---, *Fortune,* April 15, 2002, pp. F-1 to F-71 (lists of 500 largest corporations in the U.S. ranked by revenue).

---, *Forbes,* April 15, 2002, pp. 144-202 (lists of top 500 companies in the U.S. ranked by sales, profits, assets, and market value).

---, *Trade Happens: Free or Fair?...Global Challenges, Local Realities,* sponsored by the Madison Fair Trade Action Alliance, April 26-27, 2002, Madison, Wisconsin.

---, "Learn from Lands' End," editorial, *The Capital Times,* May 15, 2002c.

❧ *Subject Index* ❧

෴

Order Form

Order Form

Item	Price	Quantity	Total
Business Decisions (ISBN 0-9721875-0-2; softcover; 224 pages)	15.95 X	_____ =	_____
shipping (add $4.00 for first book, then $2.00/book)		=	_____
SUB-TOTAL		=	_____
plus sales tax (add 5.5% for Wisconsin orders)		=	_____
TOTAL AMOUNT DUE		=	_____

Please make check payable to: QUARTER SECTION PRESS

Name _____

Mailing address _____

City _____ State _____ ZIP_____

Phone _____ Email _____

Mail order to:

QUARTER SECTION PRESS
a unit of Eriksson Research, LLC
6105 Fairfax Lane
Madison, WI 53718-8262 U.S.A.

608.222.2689 - erikssonresearch@execpc.com
www.execpc.com/~erikres - www.madisonconsultants.com

QUARTER SECTION PRESS
a unit of Eriksson Research, LLC